Dear Jed,

To Mississippi Metal
Recycling with my
Best regards!
Mike

SUPER CARGO SHIPS

Christopher Batio

MBI Publishing Company

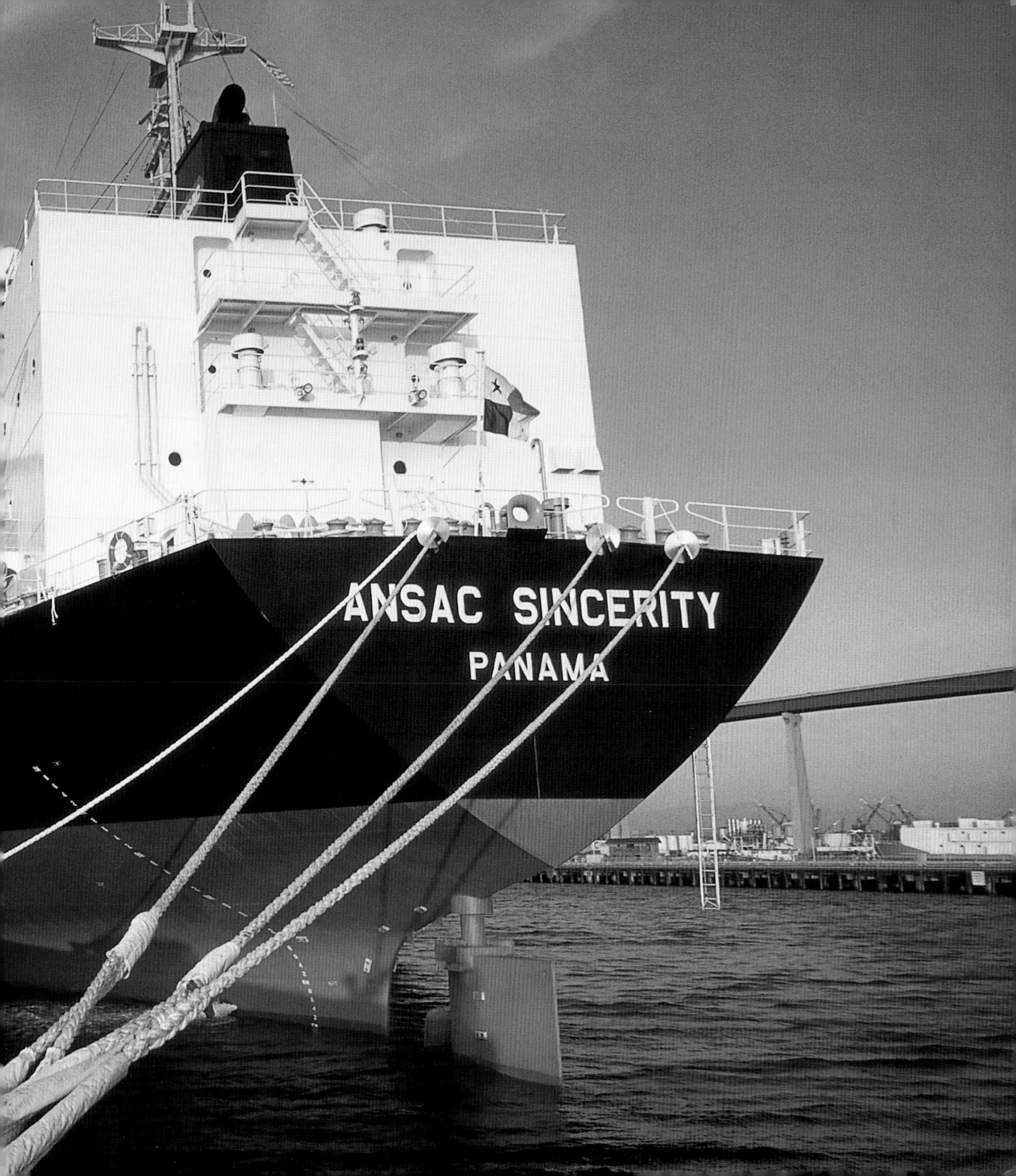
ANSAC SINCERITY
PANAMA

First published in 2001 by MBI Publishing Company, 729 Prospect Avenue, PO Box 1, Osceola, WI 54020-0001 USA

MBI Publishing Company books are also available at discounts in bulk quantity for industrial or sales-promotional use. For details write to Special Sales Manager at Motorbooks International Wholesalers & Distributors, 729 Prospect Avenue, PO Box 1, Osceola, WI 54020-0001 USA.

Library of Congress Cataloging-in-Publication Data available

On the cover: *Stena Convoy* riding high under ballast. This ship, built in 1972, was one of the first VLCCs built above 250,000 DWTs. Her twin helicopter pads and the manifold system that facilitates loading are clearly visible. *Stena AB*

On the title page: When a ship is tied up in port, the concealed parts of a ship, such as the rudder, can be inspected and repaired. While the ship is docked, the engineering team has time to perform routine maintenance and make the necessary repairs that are not possible at sea. *Port of San Diego*

Frontis: The *Cape Blanco* and *Cape Borda* are two break bulk ships that sail as part of the United States' Military Sealift Command. Their job is to move supplies and equipment around the globe for the U.S. military.

Back Cover: The Liberty Ship was a practical design that could pay for itself in just two voyages, and more than 2,700 were built to carry supplies during World War II. *Jeremiah O'Brien* and *John W. Brown*, shown here, are the only two unmodified Liberty ships still afloat. Today they serve as living museums on the west and east coasts of the USA.

Edited by Steve Hendrickson
Designed by Bruce Leckie

Printed in China

Contents

CHAPTER ONE

Highways of the Sea

Since the age of ancient Greece, the seas have carried the life's blood of the world's economy. Trading ships of the Phoenicians, Vikings, and Chinese carried goods and resources far beyond the local villages, cities, and kingdoms of origin.

As the mariners explored new waters and traded their goods for strange and curious items that they found, bartered for, or captured, the world of commerce began. Knowledge and use of an item fed a desire for more, which led to trade and contact. This contact led to the urge to learn and explore, which has brought us through the many years of history to the present.

The simple act of loading goods and people onto a ship and heading for the far horizon was one of the basic building blocks of our civilization. Today commercial shipping remains the most efficient and common way to move products and resources from one nation to another.

The cargo ship has gone through many incarnations over the years. The Viking longboat, Dutch carrack, British East Indiaman, and

The SS *Great Britain* was the first iron-hulled, propeller-driven steamship in the world. Launched in 1843, she was the forerunner of all modern cargo ships. She survives today and is being restored in Bristol, England. *SS Great Britain Project*

The oil tanker, *Kara Sea*, is shown tied up to the oil/ gasoline facility at the junction of the Napa and Sacramento Rivers in October 1999. At the junction of the Sacramento Delta and San Francisco Bay, a large number of petroleum refineries and tanker loading and unloading stations have been established. *Courtesy Kit Bonner*

the American clipper each represent a great leap forward in shipping technology. The forerunner of all modern cargo ships plying today's ocean highways is the SS *Great Britain*. How fitting that it is named after the nation that has used the seas to greater advantage than any other nation.

In 1843 the SS *Great Britain* combined all three of the major technical innovations that made modern cargo ships possible: a steam engine, iron hull, and screw propeller. The ship's designer was Isambard Kingdom Brunel, a visionary English engineer and architect who helped build the first tunnel under the Thames River.

Although the ship carried five masts and sails, the *Great Britain* was mainly powered by a screw propeller, which could move it through ocean waves much more efficiently than the paddle wheels that

steam-engined ships had used since their invention by Robert Clermont in 1807. The ship's iron hull was much stronger than a wooden hull of the same dimensions and eliminated the need for extensive internal bulkheads and braces. For this reason, the SS *Great Britain* could carry much more cargo than a wooden ship.

The ship spent much of its career carrying cargo and immigrants to Australia. It could make the trip there and back in 120 days. In 1970 the SS *Great Britain* was rescued from a beach in the Falkland Islands where it had been slowly decaying for 50 years. It was towed to Bristol, England, where it remains today, restored and on display as an example of early shipping innovation.

Brunel's practice of combining innovative ideas with new technologies paved the way for each advancement in shipping since the mid-1800s. The conservative owners and operators of ships often wait decades to adopt what appear to be obvious improvements. It took nearly 80 years for the combination of steam and propeller to completely supplant the sailing ships that had dominated the seas.

Changes occurred in the commercial shipping market throughout the twentieth century. The introduction of the container ship in 1956 by trucking tycoon Malcolm McLean was another breakthrough event, not in ship construction, but in use. His vision was to place an entire truck container on a ship deck intact. This eliminated the time-consuming action of unloading goods from trucks, moving them onto pallets or netting, and then loading them by crane into the hold of a conventional freighter. Instead the goods remained locked inside a steel truck container,

The *Western Sea*, a K-Line car carrier, slowly makes her way to the mouth of the Columbia River in this photo from June 2000. The box-like vessel has just passed beneath the bridge connecting Astoria, Oregon, to Washington State across the river. This purpose-built vessel will pass through the Columbia River Bar to escape to the open sea. *Courtesy Kit Bonner*

The *Stellar Stream* is moored in the Port of Vancouver, British Columbia. This vessel is built to carry a variety of cargoes ranging from wood chips to ore. The Stellar Stream is one of the thousands of bulkers that sail the seas. These diesel-powered ships represent the modern-day version of the early twentieth century tramp steamers. *Courtesy Kit Bonner*

which was picked up and loaded onto the ship intact. The new system made loading and unloading 20 times faster.

As McLean's idea of containerization was accepted and spread, his SeaLand company grew and prospered. Specialized container ships were designed, built, and improved. It took nearly 30 years for containers to become the dominant and ubiquitous force in shipping that they are today. Like many previous advances, the rise of the container ship caused other types of ships to change and adapt as well.

Nearly every ship has had to become larger and faster to compete with such an efficient system. General cargo ships with the typical configuration of a central bridge, with forward and rear holds, have nearly faded from existence. Specialized bulk vessels with massive sliding hatches carry the shrinking amount of cargo that cannot be containerized.

RO/RO ships (cargo ships or ferries with facilities for vehicles to drive on and off—roll-on/roll-off—via a system of ramps), many of which also carry containers on the top deck, have completely changed the shipping of vehicles. No longer does a car or truck need to fly on a crane to find a place in the ship's hold. Today it can simply be driven on board and parked in the massive innards of a specially designed "floating garage."

Even as ship designs have changed, some of the dangers that commercial ships must face on the oceans and seas have not. In the age of sail, vessels carrying spices, gold, and exotic goods from Asia and the Americas had to be well armed and sturdy to defend themselves from pirates and privateers of rival nations. Although the defensive capability of today's ships is mostly limited to small arms kept locked in the captain's cabin, sailors on the seas of the twenty-first century must

Most modern, high-volume cargo ports employ specially-designed container loading and unloading facilities for ships such as the *Sea Jaguar*, seen here in Norfolk, Virginia, in August 1998. There is a huge fleet of container ships operating worldwide. Entire ports, including those in Long Beach, California, and Sydney, Australia, are employed to take advantage of the phenomenal amount of diverse cargo that ships, like the *Sea Jaguar*, can carry. *Courtesy Kit Bonner*

still contend with pirates. In lawless areas of the world, such as the African coast, Indonesia, and the South China Sea, pirates still exist. They approach a slow-moving freighter navigating through a remote place, send boarders onto the vessel, and overwhelm the crew with knives and guns. Since most commercial ships today carry fewer than 30 crew members, it is easier for modern pirates to take over a ship.

In February 2000, a Japanese bulk freighter carrying timber from Malaysia was hijacked. The ship and crew were missing for three weeks before the captain and his men were finally discovered adrift in a small disabled boat. The crew had been forced off the ship by pirates. The modern buccaneers likely altered the ship's appearance, sailed it to a port in China or Indonesia to sell the cargo, and possibly sold the vessel as well. The stolen ship and cargo may never be found.

Another revolution in shipping, and some say it is a bad one, has been the growing use of "flags of convenience" by ship owners. Many people visiting a port or taking a cruise for the first time are surprised to see so many ships flying the flags of tiny nations such as Panama, Liberia, and Malta. These small countries are not flush with wealthy shipping magnates; they are havens for ship owners seeking a low-cost regulation for their vessels.

Since the oceans belong to everyone and national laws end 3 miles from the coast, a ship's flag is a way of indicating what nation's laws govern its operation. Until the 1970s it was common for ships to fly the flag that corresponded with the nationality of their owner or the home of the corporation that controlled them. American owners operated American-flagged ships, and British companies operated ships flying the Union Jack. In return, the regulating nation earned fees for licensing the ship.

Opposite: Intermodality has always been the goal of cargo shippers, but in the past bundles and pallets had to move from the hold to the railroad car with the help of several cranes and dozens of workers. Of course, damage to the cargo was often the unfortunate result. *Author's collection*

The triple-expansion steam engine found in steamships has nearly disappeared from the seas today, but in 1900, these engines were at the height of technology. Because of its simplicity and reliability, this engine was chosen to power the Liberty Ships of World War II. *Project Liberty Ship*

Liberty Ships

Jeremiah O'Brien and *John W. Brown* are the only two unmodified Liberty Ships still afloat. Today they serve as living museums on the West and East Coasts of the United States. *Project Liberty Ship*

During World War II when German U-boats were sinking Allied ships faster than they could be built, American shipyards built a cargo ship that literally saved Great Britain from starvation. The Liberty Ship was a super ship—not in size but in concept. It could be built cheaply, quickly, and in great numbers to deliver cargo nearly anywhere in the world.

The story begins in the autumn of 1940. The battle of the Atlantic was raging and it looked like the U-boat was going to strangle Britain's vital ocean lifelines. President Franklin Roosevelt had already transferred 50 American destroyers to the British, and the Lend-Lease Act giving Britain free access to war materiel was months away. Goods would soon be pouring out of North American factories, but ships were needed to transfer the goods to Europe.

Members of the British Shipbuilding Commission toured a number of shipbuilding and engineering facilities in the United States and

Canada. They were looking for someone who could supply new ships in a hurry. Henry J. Kaiser was the man.

In 1940, Kaiser was already well known in America. In 25 years he had built one of the largest construction and engineering firms in the world and tackled projects such as building the Hoover Dam and the Oakland Bay Bridge. The British negotiated a contract with a syndicate formed by the Todd Shipbuilding Corporation and Kaiser. It called for 60 tramp steamers with 10,000-ton deadweight capacities to be built. The vessels' configuration was based on a British design that Kaiser and his engineers modified to be easily constructed.

Kaiser and his group used modular construction techniques that allowed many sections of the ships to be built in different parts of the shipyard by inexperienced laborers. They also made the mechanical systems on the ship as simple as possible so conscripted sailors could operate the Liberty Ship with a minimum amount of training. For example, the Liberty Ship was powered by a triple-expansion steam plant that was obsolete before World War II began. First designed in 1879, this engine was rugged and easy to maintain.

The total cost of the British order was nearly $96 million, and the bill was paid in cash. Thirty vessels were built in Portland, Maine, and 30 were built in Kaiser's brand-new Permanente Yard in Richmond, California. Twenty-six more ships were built in Canada, giving a needed boost to Britain's

merchant marines. This was just the beginning.

On January 3, 1941, President Roosevelt announced a $350-million shipbuilding program to expand America's merchant fleet. The program was full speed ahead by September 27, 1941, when the first American Liberty Ship, the *Patrick Henry*, was launched in Baltimore. Even though some people called them "rolling tubs" or "ugly ducklings," the vessels were most commonly known as Liberty Ships.

During the next four years, American shipyards built enough ships to equal half the number of all of the world's prewar merchant shipping—more than 2,700 were Liberty Ships. Each Liberty Ship was 441 feet long with a 57-foot beam. The five holds (three forward of the bridge, two aft) could hold about 10,000 tons of cargo. The ship traveled at a top speed of 11 knots, and for protection, carried one 5-inch gun, three 3-inch guns, and eight 20-millimeter Oerlikon anti-aircraft guns.

Each Liberty Ship cost $1.75 million to build, but it was felt that if the ship could make more than one trip, it would be cost effective. Luckily, the Battle of the Atlantic swung to the Allied side, and only 196 Liberties were lost in combat. Approximately half of the surviving fleet was sold at the end of the war. Some of those ships were still in service 25 years later.

Today, only two Liberty Ships survive—the *John W. Brown* in Baltimore, Maryland, and the *Jeremiah O'Brien* in San Francisco, California. Both ships have been restored to wartime condition, are open for tours, and make occasional cruises in local waters.

Many freighters used to carry passengers and cargo on a regular basis to locations near and far. This ship was operated by the Alaskan Steam Ship Company for more than 20 years and ran between Seattle, Washington, and Juneau, Alaska. *Author's collection*

National merchant fleets are extremely important in many ways. They not only carry the goods of a nation in peaceful times, but they transport arms and resources in times of war. In addition, merchant fleets can be an important source of national income since the fees paid by foreign shippers add to a nation's export revenue. Since the national merchant fleets of most countries are, in fact, owned by corporations and private citizens intent on making a profit, the interests of the government cannot be paramount. Ship owners compete in a global market and must carefully match the cost and efficiency of building and operating an American ship with rivals flying the flag of Greece, Liberia, or Costa Rica.

American-flagged ships are some of the safest afloat because of the strict safety regulations to which they must adhere. These laws are enforced by the Coast Guard and the American Bureau of Shipping. In addition, American crews are among the most experienced and the highest paid in the world. All of these facts lead to the difficult reality that a Liberian-flagged ship, with lax regulation and small requirement for an experienced crew, can usually underbid an American ship competing for trade. One clear exception is called "cabotage." This is the practice of shipping goods by sea from port to port within a nation. In most countries this internal trade is reserved exclusively for vessels flying the national flag. Until the 1930s this trade was an important factor in bolstering the American merchant fleet, but today the size and efficiency of the internal roads and rails in the United States have limited cabotage activity.

Many nations subsidize the cost of maintaining their national merchant fleets. The United States did so until Ronald Reagan deeply curtailed these subsidies during his presidency in the 1980s. The U.S. merchant fleet has been shrinking ever since. In fact, most of the materiel shipped to the Middle East during the Persian Gulf War was carried on foreign-flagged vessels.

Some economists believe America is so important in the world economy that we do not need to subsidize a national merchant fleet. They theorize that ship owners must serve our ports or lose too great a portion of their business; however, the U.S. Congress was concerned enough about the nation's sealift capacity to approve funds to build dozens of new fast military cargo ships in the 1990s.

The Victory Ship was an improvement over the basic World War II Liberty Ship. Its streamlined bow and diesel engines offered significant performance gains. Many ships, including this one, were converted to troop ships to bring soldiers home to America. *Author's collection*

CHAPTER TWO

The Shipyard

If the RMS *Titanic* had been built in the same manner as the Polar *Endeavour*, it wouldn't have sunk. If the *Exxon Valdez* had a hull like the latest supertanker being built at the Litton-Avondale shipyard in Louisiana, Prince William Sound might still be the pristine waterway it was before 10.8 million gallons of Alaskan crude oil were spilled into it on March 24, 1989.

The *Titanic* did sink, and in the aftermath of that tragedy, improved ships and safer methods of operating them evolved. The same thing happened in the wake of the *Exxon Valdez* and the environmental damage it caused. With the Oil Pollution Control Act of 1990 (OPCA), the U.S. Congress mandated that all tankers carrying crude oil to American ports be equipped with an inner and outer hull.

With a vote and the stroke of a pen, Congress and the president made an entire class of oil tankers obsolete. Bad for the shipping companies but a boon for American shipyards such as Litton-Avondale, which at the time of the writing, is building three new double-hulled crude oil carriers brimming with the latest in maritime technology.

One of the most important features for an oil tanker is the pumping system responsible for loading and unloading the vessel. In this photo, the core of this system is shown behind one of the rear transverse bulkheads. In addition, the twin engine rooms are beginning to take shape at the stern of the ship. *Litton-Avondale*

A ship is built more in the manner of a building rather than a car or airplane. Most of the work is done outside in all kinds of weather, with only long, open workshops to shelter various cutting, stamping, and rolling machines that assist the workers. *Litton-Avondale*

The Millennium-class tankers are impressive in every way and meet or exceed all U.S. and international standards for mechanical operation and environmental safety. The ships are equipped with two main engines, each with half the horsepower of a conventional single engine. The engine rooms are separated by a fireproof, watertight bulkhead. Each engine drives a separate, controllable reversible-pitch propeller that can go from full ahead to full reverse in seconds. There are also two rudders instead of one, and each has a redundant steering system. The 12 cargo tanks have a total capacity of more than 1 million barrels of oil. Each tank is surrounded by a double skin of steel and are placed 10

This is a photo of the first *Millennium*-class tanker, the Polar *Endeavour*, almost four months into construction at the Avondale shipyard in Louisiana. This view, with the bow forward, clearly shows the ship's double hull and segregated cargo tanks. *Litton-Avondale*

feet apart. They are rated at 125,000 deadweight tonnage (DWT), the maximum legal weight for ships passing through Puget Sound.

At 895 feet long, the Polar ships use 8,000 more tons of steel than conventional ships of similar size. They're designed to have an operating life of 30 years, 10 to 20 years longer than most tankers in service today. Equipped with state-of-the-art navigational systems, the ship's bridge has electronic chart displays, three collision-avoidance radars, and the Global Marine Distress and Safety System. A single control lever, rather than several different controls, operates the propellers, rudders, and bow thrusters.

Polar *Endeavour* is the first Millennium-class ship and was delivered in July 2000. The others, Polar *Resolution* and Polar *Discovery,* will debut in early 2001 and 2002, respectively. South Korean and Japanese shipyards are currently building

The sheer size of the Polar Millennium tanker project is well illustrated by this photo of the ship's emerging superstructure. Here we see the longitudinal bulkhead that rises on the vessel's centerline to separate the starboard and port cargo tanks and give the ship strength and stability. *Litton-Avondale*

bigger tankers, with some reaching up to 300,000 DWT. Only one Swedish company, N&T Argonaut, is building tankers with comparable standards for safety.

In the United States, Litton-Avondale is consistently turning out some of the largest and most sophisticated commercial and military ships built today. In fact, the company is the only American

Several mobile cranes stand ready to service the Polar *Endeavour* job site. Lateral stiffeners and hull components at the bottom right will be moved into place and welded securely to the hull. *Litton-Avondale*

shipyard that has recently produced nearly every major type of commercial ship from tankers and RO/ROs to LASH ships and bulk carriers. On the banks of the Mississippi River near New Orleans, these massive ships, produced from scratch, come together with steel and sweat.

Every shipbuilding project follows certain steps. Number one is determining the customer's requirements for the final product. With the Millennium tankers, Congress dictated how the ship must operate and what it must do when OPCA was signed. The law was clear on the features required for tankers calling on U.S. ports.

The second step is design. For these tankers, the process of deciding how big the vessel will be, what hull form to use, and the engine and speed requirements was accomplished by a New Ship Build Team assembled from Polar Marine's staff of naval architects, marine engineers, project managers, and cost coordinators. They formed

Opposite and Above: The construction of the Polar *Endeavour* proceeds forward and aft. At the ship's bow, the starboard and port bulkheads curve inward with the ballast spaces visible between the inner and outer hull. At the stern, twin driveshafts will soon be installed in the starboard and port tunnels near the hull bottom. *Litton-Avondale*

the performance specs and basic design and worked with Litton-Avondale's own design team to bring the Millennium tanker to life on paper and on the computer.

Once the design was complete, it had to be reviewed by the American Bureau of Shipping (ABS)—the classification society responsible for approving all American ship designs. Classification societies originally assessed the risk of insuring a vessel, but now they are more involved in regulating safe conditions and construction of vessels built in the major shipbuilding nations. Some overseas classification societies include Lloyd's Register of Shipping in Britain, Norway's Det Norske Veritas, and

Major shipyards, such as Litton-Avondale, manufacture almost every part of the ship. Rudders are produced in this shop. For added safety, every Polar Millennium ship will have two rudders. *Litton-Avondale*

Japan's Nippon Kaigi Ngokai. Once ABS gave approval to the design, construction began. It takes two years to build each Millennium tanker.

The Litton-Avondale shipyard covers hundreds of acres along the riverfront in steamy Metarie, Louisiana. The site consists of several low-roofed workshops and open drydocks turning raw steel I-beams and plates into towering ships that almost seem to live and breathe. The

steel is delivered to the yard on rail flatcars that find their way onto the site across an immense rail bridge that literally dominates the skyline for miles around. Bug-like utility crawlers pick up the steel beams and stack them into long piles until they are needed at the cutting sheds. In these sheds, the top (and sometimes the bottom) of the I-beam is cut off lengthwise so a "T" or an "I" is what remains. Men feed the steel

Nearly one year into its construction, the Polar *Endeavour* is beginning to look like what it will become—a massive and modern oil tanker. *Litton-Avondale*

into the cutting machine like logs being turned into planks.

Steel plates are processed in a similar fashion, and large sections are cut and shaped according to the needs of each ship part. Very little steel is wasted. Different sections of the beams and plates are moved from the cutting shed to a welding area where they are placed on pin jigs to be fashioned into the bones of the ship. Plates are welded to beams to make

boxes, panels, stiffeners, and bulkheads. With increasing speed, each section takes shape.

Years ago, ships were built from the keel up on a slipway, similar to a puzzle being completed one piece at a time. Today engineers at Avondale and other shipyards have perfected the process to build whole sections of the ship in different parts of the yard and bring each modular unit together to be welded and bolted into place. The pieces are assembled on a

As construction continues, the deck catwalk and bridge are taking shape. The lines snaked all over the tanker's top deck carry welding gas and electricity to various construction stations. *Author's collection*

carriage that moves laterally from the yard to the edge of the Mississippi River and then onto a huge floating drydock. In this manner, several ships can be assembled at the same time.

Engines, driveshafts, screws, and rudders are installed. In the bowels of the ship, cargo and ballast tanks take shape along with the piping and equipment needed to load and unload them. Once the hull is completely fabricated and watertight, the drydock is lowered, water floods in, and the hull floats. The ship is towed to a "fitting-out" dock for installation of the interiors, as well as the steering, fire control, and navigation systems.

Litton-Avondale manufactures the hull and superstructure of the ship, but it acquires different components such as engines, electronics, crew cabins, and fire-suppression equipment from outside vendors. Each of these items is incorporated into the design of the ship and installed into the hull at predetermined points during the construction.

During a recent visit to the Avondale yard, there were three tankers in various stages of construction; a new Coast Guard icebreaker returning from sea trials; two military sealift ships under construction, and one more being prepared for delivery to the Military Sealift Command.

Most industrialized countries regard shipbuilding technology as a vital national resource. Shipyards are often supported by the government as a means to provide the nation with military and economic status on the ocean. For example, in March 2000 Vietnam banned the importation of any ship that could be built by that nation's shipyards. This was a way to spur production and growth of the country's domestic shipbuilding capacity.

Shipbuilding was once one of the most important industries in the United States. It formed the basis of several family fortunes and employed tens of thousands of workers on the East, West, and Gulf Coasts. Today only six American shipyards,

When the Polar *Endeavour* becomes operational, its cargo will be pumped aboard and unloaded via the piping manifolds running from the vessel's centerline to the edge of the top deck. *Litton-Avondale*

controlled by three corporations, exist that can truly build nearly any type of commercial or military vessel. They are Litton-Avondale in Metarie, Louisiana; General Dynamics Bath Iron Works in Bath, Maine; General Dynamics Electric Boat in Groton, Connecticut; Litton-Ingalls Shipbuilding in Pascagoula, Mississippi; General Dynamics NASSCO in San Diego, California; and Newport News Shipbuilding in Newport News, Virginia.

Bath, Litton-Ingalls, Newport News, and Electric Boat are generally military shipyards and build escort ships, submarines, and aircraft carriers. NASSCO and Litton-Avondale perform a mix of military and commercial work. Several smaller American shipyards stay busy building tugs, fishing boats, and medium-sized commercial vessels.

One of the brightest developments in American shipbuilding is the Kvaerner Philadelphia project, which is seeking to turn the old Philadelphia Naval Shipyard into a viable commercial yard. Work has already begun on a new 30,000-DWT container ship. Despite this project, much of the shipbuilding business has gravitated to Asia during the last 30 years.

Since 1970 the top shipbuilding nations in the world have been Japan and South Korea. Their large and efficient yards have turned out every type of commercial ship afloat; however, the Korean yards especially have been accused of dumping ship tonnage on the world market by building ships at a loss. This may have been done to gain market share and to keep the incredible capacity of the Hyundai, Daewoo, and Samsung yards operating at sustainable levels.

The result has been a decrease in the price of used ships and an increase in the number of old, and not so old, ships being broken up for scrap. Recently, Chinese shipyards have been building a market share of their own, leading to the speculation about what nation will be the next great shipbuilder to emerge in Asia. Vietnam and India are the most likely candidates.

Even in the face of this competition, shipyards around the world have been increasingly busy. As Western Europe's shipbuilders have seen their market share erode, European yards that are unable to compete with price have been obliged to specialize and focus their expertise on gas and chemical tankers and cruise ships. Most modern cruise ships

This is what the finished product will look like. The *Millennium*-class tanker is one of the most advanced vessels afloat. *Litton-Avondale*

Ships are built in stages, and as work progresses at Avondale, the ship moves closer and closer to being launched in the floating dry dock at right. Once the military RO/RO shown here is floated and moved to the outfitting dock for installation of its electronics and detail work, the next ship in line will be moved to the right on a system of removable rails that bridge the gaps between each construction area. *Litton-Avondale*

are produced in Italy, Germany, or Finland. American yards make the most sophisticated military vessels afloat. Danish and German yards have also produced some of the largest container ships. Asian yards have special expertise as well. China has been making more of the world's bulkers. Most of the liquid natural gas tankers in the world have been made in South Korea or Japan. Japanese yards continue to produce many of the largest and best tankers around, and India has nearly cornered the market on "breaking" or scrapping ships.

This military sealift ship, the USNS *Mendonca,* is ready for launch in the dry dock. It will be lowered into the water and towed downstream to have the final touches put on the ship. *Litton-Avondale*

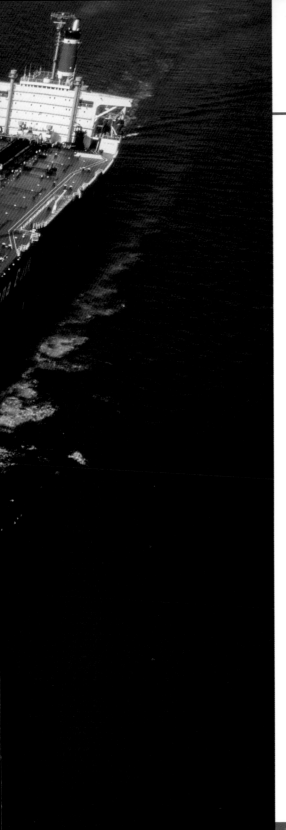

CHAPTER THREE

Oil and Gas Tankers

The fact is that now, and for the foreseeable future, the world cannot run without oil. All transportation depends, in some form, on petroleum for gasoline, diesel fuel, aviation gas, bunker oil, propane, and the natural gas that powers most electrical plants. All of these products move across the globe in a delicate web of interlacing sea-lanes, truck routes, and pipelines. The ocean leg of this network is by far the most important.

Nearly half of the world's ocean trade consists of ships carrying oil and petroleum products. Of course when most people think of an oil tanker, they imagine an immense ship filled to the brim with sticky black oil pumped raw from the Earth. In actuality, most tankers are smaller and more sophisticated and specialized than that.

Oil has been useful for centuries, but it has become the driving force of the world's economy in the last century. Ancient humans used oil tar and pitch (found in sandpits and swamps) to build roads, make medicine, and seal ship hulls. In 1859 America invented the petroleum industry when Edwin Drake drilled the first oil well 60 feet into the ground at Titusville, Pennsylvania. Drake coined the word *petroleum* by taking the Greek words for rock (*petra*) and the Latin word for oil (*oleum*) and mashing them together.

Stena Constellation riding high under ballast. This VLCC ship, built in 1975, has 6 center tanks and 10 wing tanks for hauling cargo. Her twin helicopter pads and the manifold system that facilitates loading are clearly visible. *Stena AB*

33

One of the most important components on any oil tanker is the cargo loading/offloading system made up of these pipes, joints and manifolds. The system is constructed so the tanker can carry several different grades of oil or refined fuel. Each cargo type will be loaded and unloaded by a separate set of pipes to avoid product contamination.

The Eagle *Auriga* is a double-hulled tanker built in 1993 for American Eagle Tankers, a subsidiary of Neptune Orient Lines. This ship carries crude oil from Venezuela and Mexico to U.S. refineries. Here she enters the Port of New Orleans with a load of cargo. *Port of New Orleans/Donn Young*

Clean-burning "rock oil" quickly replaced sooty fuels gained from whale blubber or coal. Within one year of Drake's first well, 16 oil refineries had sprouted up nearby, and by 1861, Philadelphia was exporting its main products, kerosene and lubricating oil, to Europe and points beyond.

Kerosene was first shipped in barrels packed into conventional cargo brigs. By 1864 these products were the nation's sixth largest export item. The trade would likely have been greater if more ship owners could have been persuaded to carry the dangerous cargo. Barrels were notoriously leaky and their round shape wasted valuable cargo space in the hold that could not be filled by any other cargo that was edible or flammable. Clearly oil products needed to be carried on a special ship.

After several smaller and less than successful attempts, the first ship designed to carry petroleum

exclusively was the *Gluckauf*, a 2,300-ton coal-fired steamer built in England during 1886. Its iron hull had a center bulkhead along the keel and eight transverse bulkheads to create 16 separate tanks. This segregated the cargo and reduced the surface action of the oil as the ship moved. It also reduced the inherent instability of filling a ship with a liquid cargo.

In the years that followed, tankers grew in size and sophistication. Some of the innovations introduced included duplicate loading and offloading pipework to allow carriage of different types of oil products in one ship. Safe tank venting was also a necessary discovery, and fuel oil and diesel was introduced as a logical replacement for coal to power the tanker engines.

As World War II began, the United States introduced a new tanker design, the T2. It was the tanker equivalent of a Liberty Ship—easy to build, operate,

The *Chevron Arizona* is a double-hull product carrier built in 1977. Here, she's being docked by two tugs in Mobile, Alabama. *Bill Burt*

and maintain. The T2 could carry 16,000 tons of oil products in segregated tanks that could handle crude or refined fuels. This basic tanker was built in vast numbers and sold for little more than scrap once the war was over. The T2 formed the basis of several postwar shipping empires.

Until World War II, tankers carried more refined products than crude oil. This occurred mainly because most refineries had been built close to the world's main oil fields in the United States, Russia, and the Persian Gulf. After the war the industrial nations of the world needed more fuel than ever to power their growing economies; however, growth in fuel demand, the need for a greater variety of different fuels, and a slow drop in domestic oil production made most Western countries into oil importers.

Crude now fills the ocean pipeline to feed the demand at refineries in the United States and Europe. Most of the new oil comes from the Middle East. This basic trend has continued with only two major deviations in the past 40 years, the oil embargo of the mid-1970s and the discovery of new oil resources in Alaska and the North Sea.

Despite conservation gains and the use of these new resources, the American trend toward the use of more and more imported oil continues, and the tanker trade is affected through the need for more tankers and diverse ships to keep the ocean pipeline in operation. In February 1999, total U.S. oil production was about 600,000 barrels less than the year before. Due to the combination of low production and higher oil consumption, nearly 60 percent of U.S. oil consumption now consists of imported oil. This is an increase of more than 10 percent since 1997.

The vast variety of petroleum ships can be organized and categorized by size or cargo. For example, tankers may carry crude oil, refined petroleum products (gasoline), natural gas (methane), or refined petroleum gas (propane or butane). Tankers that carry oil and refined products are much different in design and structure from those that carry gas.

Gas tankers operate where pipelines do not exist and are not practical to build. One small but busy trade delivers gas to Caribbean islands, but the greatest gas trade operates between the Persian Gulf and energy-poor, but development-rich, nations of the Far East. As a consequence, most LPG/LNG tankers have been built in Korea or Japan. There is also a significant movement of LNG from Alaska to Japan.

The spherical or multicellular tanks of a gas carrier appear as domes or elongated prisms jutting above the tanker's deck. Natural gas is shipped in supercooled, pressurized tanks to keep the gas liquefied. In this manner, more gas can be shipped and the cargo is much less volatile. Petroleum gas is also shipped under pressure but does not need to be cooled.

Product carriers transport refined oil products such as gasoline. These ships look similar to a crude carrier on the outside but are much more sophisticated on the inside with completely segmented tanks serviced by dedicated loading and offloading pumps that will not mix products. Most military tankers can be classified as product carriers since they primarily carry refined fuels for the fleet.

HMI *Petrochem*, a chemical and oil carrier, undergoes maintenance in a floating dry dock in Mobile, Alabama. The ship's primary job is transporting refined gasoline from Texas refineries to a distribution center at the port of Tampa Bay, Florida. *Bill Burt*

The size of a supertanker — the *Stena Queen*, in this case — is deceptive since, when fully loaded, virtually all of the scarlet hull is hidden below the waterline. When the ship has unloaded its cargo and is returning to the oil fields most of the crew is occupied with maintenance. The empty cargo tanks are filled with inert gas to eliminate any possibility of explosive reactions. *Stena AB*

Crude oil carriers are organized by size. Ultra Large Crude Carriers (ULCC) are the largest tankers afloat and encompass any tanker of 350,000 dead-weight tons or more. These ships were mainly built in the early 1970s when economies of scale dictated larger and larger tankers. Changes in oil prices, accidents, and the sheer cost of operation have led ULCCs to fall out of favor with shipping owners.

Few ULCCs still operate, and even fewer are built today. These immense ships can be handled by few ports and most often unload their cargo into a floating pipeline attached to a buoy 1 or 2 miles offshore. One of the most important offshore oil-load-

ing facilities is the Louisiana Offshore Oil Port, located 18 miles off the coast of Louisiana near the mouth of the Mississippi River. It can handle 1.2 million barrels of oil per day at three separate mooring buoys. When an offshore loading facility is not available, supertankers can also be unloaded using shuttle tankers steaming alongside. This procedure is slower and more prone to oil spills than using a loading facility, however.

The Very Large Crude Carrier (VLCC) is more common today. It ranges from 200,000 to 350,000 DWT. VLCCs are the largest ships that regularly call at American ports. On a typical voyage from the

Persian Gulf to America's oil ports on the Gulf of Mexico, a VLCC will load its tanks with crude, travel southwest through the Indian Ocean, around the Cape of Good Hope, run north through the Atlantic, unload, cross the Atlantic, move through the Mediterranean, sail through the Suez Canal, and then head back to the Persian Gulf to begin the cycle again. The canal is too shallow to allow VLCC tankers to traverse its waters fully loaded; however, Suezmax tankers (130,000 to 160,000 DWT) are built to navigate the canal with a full load of oil. The size of the Suezmax tanker has

Supertankers are equipped with an enormous maze of pipes, fittings, pumps, and lines to pump cargo and ballast in and out of the cargo tanks. Maintaining this equipment is a full-time job for the ship's crew. *Stena AB*

Super Tugs

The *Exxon Valdez* disaster produced changes in how tankers and tugs that assist the tankers are built. In February 1999, Alyeska Pipeline Company took delivery of *Nanuq*, the first tug in a two-boat class built by Crowley Marine of Seattle.

The Prince William Sound ships are the largest and most versatile escort tugs ever constructed. They are designed to avert disasters similar to the *Exxon Valdez* spill and render assistance if a spill or fire does occur. One Crowley manager called it "the Swiss Army knife of tugboats."

Both Prince William Sound–class tugs are 155 feet long with two Voith Schneider cycloidal drives that extend down from the hull just forward of the amidship. Their variable-angle vertical blades are mounted in two side-by-side circles and continuously rotate at 60 to 70 rpms. By adjusting the drive blade pitch, the tug is capable of maneuvering in any direction and backed with

The *Nanuq* is one of the most powerful and versatile tugboats in the world. It works in Alaska's Prince William Sound to escort tankers and prevent spills. *Crowley Marine Services*

more than 210,000 pounds of thrust delivered by two Caterpillar diesels.

Nanuq also sports some impressive safety and firefighting equipment, including two 6,600-gallon-per-minute water nozzles, two 1,800-foot oil-containment booms, an oil skimmer with on-board storage for 73,000 gallons of recovered oil, and a dispersant sprayer. Since Alaska is its operating area, Crowley added some special features to the ships, such as electrically heated deck covers, ladders, and pilothouse windows.

Although the tugs are built for escorting tankers in and out of Prince William Sound, more super tugs may be built for the Seattle area. The increase in traffic of large cargo ships and tankers in Puget Sound has many environmentally minded area residents insisting that the super tugs are needed there, but at $15 million each tugs like the *Nanuq* are expensive, and no one has stepped forward to foot the bill in Seattle.

Looking from the bow towards the supertanker's stern, you can see the central distribution manifolds with the pipes running to and from the various cargo tanks. At the stern, the ship's superstructure rises high above the deck. *Stena AB*

A small LPG tanker lies at anchor off the coast of Florida. Small tankers are used in the Carribbean to supply gas to island powerplants. *J. E. Clark*

increased over the years as the canal has been dredged and improved. This activity continues and tankers of 180,000 DWT may soon be able to traverse the Suez.

One distinct factor that led to the increased size of oil tankers is the simple economy of scale combined with improved technology. Even though a Suezmax tanker can carry three times the cargo of a World War II–era T2, the cost of building and operating the new vessel is not three times higher.

As engines became more reliable and electronic controls were introduced, fewer crew members were needed to keep the tanker running. The same holds true for modern navigation tools. This directly reduced costs and made larger tankers much more lucrative to operate.

The future of oil tankers is not really in size but in versatility. One of the most innovative uses of tankers today is the Floating Production, Storage, and Offloading (FPSO) ship. Although purpose-

Small product and chemical tankers such as *M/T Astral* occupy a crucial position in the sea trade, especially in Europe. Products that would be shipped in tanker trucks in the United States are often transported by sea in Europe. *Rederi AB Veritas Tankers*

built FPSOs are being built, these vessels are usually older, single-hull tankers that have been converted to act as floating oil rigs. There are more and more of these ships available as nations impose laws requiring oil tankers to have double hulls. For deep water finds, FPSOs are an economical replacement for the immense and expensive steel towers and platforms that were built on land and installed on the seabed to exploit oil and gas in the North Sea.

The FPSO floats at anchor above an established oil strike and is linked to the petroleum by a flexible pipeline. Oil is pumped out of the well head, which is positioned on the ocean floor and stored in the tanks of the FPSO. Smaller shuttle tankers move from the FPSO to the coast and back and carry the oil to refineries.

In recent years, a high oil price has provided a new drive to develop new oil fields in the North Sea and elsewhere. Floating production units are being used more frequently in the development of oil fields. One of the advantages of this solution compared to previous methods of oil field development is the short amount of time required from start-up to production, especially in deep waters.

In such production, shuttle tankers play a key role. There is also a possibility of future oil field development in other geographical areas outside the North Sea. Promising increases in production from marginal fields off the coast of Brazil, the U.S. Gulf, Canada, and West Africa may spur a demand for floating production units and shuttle tankers.

CHAPTER FOUR

Container Ships

Malcolm McLean changed the world, but most people have never heard of him. McLean invented the container ship—a mode of cargo transportation that dominates seaborne commerce throughout the world and has made possible much of the trade that our global economy is based on. Since the container revolution began 44 years ago, the number and variety of goods shipped around the world in these ubiquitous steel boxes has grown exponentially.

McLean's ideas revolutionized world trade and transportation, but he did not start out as a captain of industry. Few people who met him thought he was a genius. McLean began in 1931 as a truck driver and hauled vegetables, dirt, and anything else from North Carolina farms. McLean was ambitious and hardworking and managed to build a fleet of six semi-trucks in the depths of the Depression. McLean Trucking continued to expand and carried loads of textiles north to Philadelphia and New York. Although he owned the company, McLean continued to drive loads on his own. The idea that evolved into the container ship occurred to him on a run to Hoboken, New Jersey, in 1937.

The Port of New Orleans is a good place to see nearly every type of maritime commerce and activity taking place. River barges, tankers, container ships, military ships . . . all these call at this important station to load or unload the goods and material that make world commerce possible. Port of New Orleans/Donn Young

Malcolm McLean invented the container ship and revolutionized worldwide shipping with the founding of SeaLand Service in 1956. Today, a Danish corporation, A. P. Moller Group/Maersk SeaLand, is the world's largest operator of container ships. In 1999, the company acquired SeaLand from CSX Corporation. *Maersk SeaLand*

Dole Honduras is a 900 TEU container ship carrying reefer boxes. It transports bananas from Central America to Wilmington, Delaware on a round-trip weekly basis. *J.E. Clark*

As quoted in *American Heritage* magazine, McLean explains his thoughts on that day:

I had driven my trailer truck up from Fayetteville, North Carolina, with a load of cotton bales that were to go on an American export ship tied up at the dock. For one reason or another, I had to wait most of the day to deliver the bales. As I sat there, I watched all those people muscling each crate and bundle off the trucks and into the slings that would lift them into the hold of the ship. On board the ship, every sling would have to be unloaded by the stevedores and its contents put in the proper place in the hold. What a waste in time and money! Suddenly the thought occurred to me: 'Wouldn't it be great if my trailer could simply be lifted up and placed on the ship without its contents being unloaded.' That's when the seed was planted. . . .

Container shipping has reduced the number of people needed for dock work; however, skilled and experienced stevedores and crane operators are still an integral part of any efficient port. Any ship captain will admit that properly loading and unloading a ship is nearly impossible without experienced and dedicated port workers.
Port of New Orleans/Donn Young

McLean's idea was a simple one, but it would take nearly 20 years for him to implement, and like many great advances this was a cumulative effort. In 1929, a company called Sea Train Lines began using specially built ships to carry railroad cars. Other companies had also tried to adapt ferries into truck carriers for short hauls. The problem with both approaches was weight and strength—the wasted weight of carrying the wheels of a train car or truck trailer with the cargo and the lack of

The Fastest Cargo Ship

Seldom does something completely new enter an established and well-researched realm such as commercial shipping. Robert Clermont's steamship, the Liberty Ship, and the container ship were all innovations that did enter that realm, and now another revolution promises to overthrow the status quo.

These graphics show the hull form and loading equipment of the FastShip Atlantic project. *FastShip Atlantic*

By 2002, the FastShip Atlantic project will have four ships in operation that are capable of crossing the Atlantic in four days at a top sustained speed of 40 knots. That rate is twice as fast as the best container ship in operation today, and speed is the most important element in determining the profitable operation of a cargo ship since a faster ship can complete more voyages every year. The FastShips will carry containers and RO/RO cargo between specially designed loading facilities in Philadelphia and Cherbourg. Time-sensitive goods that may now be shipped by more expensive air express services are the intended market. The ships will be able to carry 1,400 TEUs of container cargo.

The FastShip has brought together several technological advances that make this leap in performance possible. The first and most important is a special hull form that cuts through waves cleanly and with less drag than a conventional hull. Some of these waves are created by the ship itself. As speed increases with a conventional hull, the waves become as long as the ship itself. If the ship tries to increase speed, the waves elongate further and the ship "squats" at the rear.

This captive wave places so much drag on the hull that the ship cannot climb up the wave and move beyond it. This limits speed; however, the FastShip hull has a deep V-shaped bow and a wide concave hollow at the stern. This produces a second wave to shorten the captive wave and allows an increase in speed.

The second advancement is less revolutionary but is just as important to the FastShip's speed. Five Kamewa water jets (the largest ever constructed) driven by Rolls-Royce gas turbines will drive the ship. Conventional propellers cannot move a ship beyond 30 knots. At this speed, low pressure on the forward surface of the screw begins to boil the surrounding water and produces "cavitation" or disruptive vibration. By contrast, the water jets become more efficient as speeds increase. The increasing pressure under the hull forces water through the channels and into the jets. This maintains high pressure in the turbine chamber and no cavitation occurs.

The turbines used to power the water jets are similar to those used on Boeing's latest airliners and modern cruise ships. They are very reliable, the parts are easy to come by, and the turbines take up much less space than a marine diesel engine able to produce the same horsepower. This means the FastShip can carry more cargo in a smaller hull. Also the turbines can be installed below the main cargo deck, and the exhausts run up the side of the ship instead of the middle. This allows containers to be loaded from the rear on lengthwise rails, and cranes are not needed.

The loading and unloading process is the third advancement of the FastShip. The FastShip can handle RO/RO cargo at any port, but to haul its capacity limit of containers across the Atlantic it needs the special cargo-loading equipment that will be built in Philadelphia and Cherbourg. FastShip will be loaded from the rear, instead of being loaded from the top, with the assistance of cranes. Containers will be mounted on diesel-electric rail frames designed by TTS Technology of Norway. The rail frames run on tracks directly into the ship, which allow the FastShip to be unloaded and loaded within four hours.

FastShip is offering a seven-day service guarantee for customers on the East Coast of the United States and Western Europe. It will also offer five- and six-day service levels in areas within 10 hours from Philadelphia and Cherbourg.

Each FastShip will be built by NASSCO in San Diego. The company has built a number of turbine-powered warships and conventionally powered sealift ships for the U.S. Navy. The FastShips and their dedicated terminals should be operational by fall 2002.

49

One drawback to the container revolution is that it has made most existing port facilities obsolete and forced most coastal cities to build large, new marshalling yards and container terminals. The facilities can build the yards or face being bypassed by shipping traffic. *Port of New Orleans/Donn Young*

strength in both structures to stand up to a lengthy sea voyage.

By 1950 McLean had built his trucking company into one of the most successful in the country, but he never forgot his idea about putting truck trailers onto ships. His first thought was to build a floating garage, similar to a modern RO/RO ship. The floating garage proved to be inefficient to compete effectively with highway shipping. McLean and his staff concluded that the truck trailer had to be removed from the chassis, able to be loaded on and off the ship quickly, and stackable.

Finally having the resources and vision to try out his ideas, McLean purchased a small operator of

oil tankers called Pan Atlantic Lines. He ordered 600 reinforced containers to be built and constructed a steel deck on which to mount the assembled containers on top of the main deck of the *Ideal X*, a T2-type oil tanker running petroleum from Houston to New York.

On its first voyage on April 26, 1956, the *Ideal X* carried 58 containers. Within one year, McLean had four ships just like her to carry oil from Texas to New York and run both ways with full containers. As the success of containerization grew more evident, the Interstate Commerce Commission forced McLean to decide between trucks and ships; he could not operate both. With typical

Once containers leave the ship, they may travel for days more before they reach the destination of their cargo, and sometimes they don't make it back to sea. In some countries containers have been turned into warehouses, emergency housing, and even a roadside cafe. *Port of New Orleans/Donn Young*

See the World from the Deck of a Cargo Ship

Taking a cruise in the Caribbean or Greek Isles has long been a popular vacation choice, but some adventurous souls want to go to sea in a different way and book passage on a cargo ship bound for uncommon ports.

If you're reading this book, you probably are already interested in freighters, but taking a trip on one may or may not be for you. The key is knowing what to expect and being flexible. Itineraries can change daily and a port you may have planned to visit could be bypassed completely. Cargo ship cruising is best suited for people who know how to entertain themselves, are comfortable in small groups, don't expect formal dining or organized activities, and want a relaxing unstructured trip.

Cargo ship voyages are rarely shorter than 20 days and often last 60 days or longer, so it helps to have more than two weeks of vacation time. One exception to this rule is transatlantic crossings on container ships. These trips can be completed in 9 or 10 days. For example, Mitsui OSK Lines can accommodate up to eight passengers on its *MOL Europe* container ship that travels from Antwerp, Belgium, to New York in 10 days for about $1,000. The cost of freighter cruises can be compared to other cruise vacations. The per-day cost is less and is often under $100 a day, but since freighter cruises usually last longer than leisure cruises the total cost of the trip is likely to be higher.

Many breakbulk and container ships carry passengers regularly, but tankers and bulk carriers rarely do. Since maritime law often requires a ship carrying more than 12 passengers to have a doctor on board, passenger space is limited on most cargo ships.

Freighter cabins are usually spacious and can include a full bath and sitting area in addition to two twin beds or lower bunks. They often come with stereos, TV/VCRs, and large windows as well. A cabin steward will be assigned to clean your room and change linens, but personal services like laundry and ironing is the passenger's responsibility. Most ships have a washer and dryer available for passengers to use.

The food on freighter cruises does not compare to the around-the-clock gourmet buffets that pervade leisure cruisers. On most freighter ships, passengers eat with the officers at set meal times for breakfast, lunch, and dinner. The cuisine will likely be simple, filling, and will probably reflect the ethnic makeup of the crew. If you are hungry in between meals, the ship's pantry is open to all. Many vessels also have a passenger lounge and a small store called a "slop chest" that sells duty-free goods. The lounge usually has a bar, small library, and table games. Other passenger spaces may include an outside deck with lounge chairs, an exercise room, sauna, or small saltwater pool.

One of the true advantages of cargo ship cruising is having extensive access to all aspects of a working ship. Maritime enthusiasts will especially enjoy regular visits to the bridge or the engine room, and there is usually plenty of time to socialize with the ship's officers during meals.

There are several good web sites that give information about cargo ship cruises. They are: The Cruise People Ltd.—members.aol.com/CruiseAZ/home.html, TravLTips—http://travltips.com, and the Internet Guide to Freighter Travel—people.we.mediaone.net/freighterman/index.html.

Breakbulk cargo cannot be containerized, so it is loaded the old-fashioned way: with a ship's crane into a bulker or general cargo vessel. *Port of New Orleans/Donn Young*

boldness, McLean sold the trucking company that had been the basis of his fortune and devoted himself full-time to what would become the SeaLand Service.

To take full advantage of containerization efficiencies, SeaLand began building ships designed to carry containers only. The first ship, *Gateway City,* was launched on October 4, 1957, and could carry 226 containers. As an illustration of how containerization could save shipping companies and their customers a great deal of money, Lane Kendall and James Buckley included the following analysis in their 1994 book, *The Business of Shipping:*

Gateway City was assigned to sail between Port Newark and Houston, a distance of 1,928 miles. At her normal cruising speed of 14.5 knots, the one way passage required 133 hours, without allowing for possible delays. In Houston, she used 14 hours to discharge and reload, and then spent 133 hours steaming back to Port Newark. Port time in the New Jersey terminal was 14 hours, bringing the total time for the round trip to 294 hours. During the 50 weeks of the operating year, the ship was able to complete 28.56 round voyages. The *Fair Isle,* a conventional breakbulk ship comparable in all performance respects to the *Gateway City,* operated

Day or night, cargo must be moved so ships can stay on schedule. Ships like the *P&O Nedloyd Caracas* use every square inch, including the stern deck behind the wheelhouse, to pack containers on board. *Port of New Orleans/Donn Young*

on the same route. Her sea time was identical to the container ship, but discharging and reloading required 84 hours in Houston and a similar time period in New Jersey. Total voyage time came to 434 hours. In 50 weeks, the *Fair Isle* completed 19.35 voyages.

Kendall and Buckley's analysis clearly demonstrates the inevitable success of container ships and why they have become so important to world trade. In addition to the inherent loading/unloading efficiency, containers also proved to be a safer way to ship sensitive or fragile cargo. All of these factors made McLean and SeaLand an unqualified success. Of course, other companies eventually followed.

The story of the container ship is more than the story of a ship. It's the story of the containers they carry. These steel boxes bring the seacoast to the driest desert on the back of a truck or train. In some remote areas, they are used as warehouses, stores, and homes. Special containers are used for carrying refrigerated goods, hanging racks of clothing, liquids, and dry bulk.

As container traffic grew, one of the first problems was to establish a standard size for the container. SeaLand had initially used a 35-foot-long box that mirrored the size of a standard truck trailer. Other companies used boxes that ranged from 10 to 40 feet long, but all containers were 8 feet wide and 8 feet high. In 1961 the International Standards Organization recommended uniform sizes based on 10-, 20-, and 40-foot lengths. The resulting standard evolved into the 20-foot equivalent unit (TEU), which is used today to designate the carrying capacity of container ships worldwide.

Initially, shipping companies owned the containers they moved. Each ship needed three sets of containers to operate effectively—one loaded with goods, one in transit, and one to be unloaded. The construction and tracking of these boxes represented a huge investment for shipping companies, which proved to be too large of an investment for some smaller companies to handle. Eventually, companies emerged with no other purpose than to own and rent containers to shipping companies. These "neutral pools" were the logical outgrowth of the burgeoning container traffic that saw SeaLand's container holdings grow from 600 in 1956 to 18,490 in 1966.

Today, container ships continue to grow larger, much as tankers did in the 1970s. Classes of container ships are referred to in Panamax and post-Panamax terms for ships that can transit the Panama canal and those that cannot. The largest ships carry more than 6,000 TEUs, and ultramax carriers of 12,500 TEUs are on the drawing board.

Shipping is an international business. Although flags of convenience are common, vessel names still offer a good indication of the ties a ship may have. This ship, the TMM *Oaxaca,* carries bulk cargo and containers for Transportacion Maritima Mexicana S.A. *Port of New Orleans/Donn Young*

CHAPTER FIVE

Military Sealift Command

America has commitments around the world. Allies depend on the United States, and have enemies to deal with.

During a war, more than 95 percent of the equipment and supplies needed to sustain the U.S. military are carried by sea. The mission of Military Sealift Command is to provide ocean transportation of equipment, fuel, supplies, and ammunition to sustain American military forces worldwide during peacetime and in war for as long as necessary.

Numerous international crises in the 1990s showed the vital role the Military Sealift Command (MSC) plays in our national strategy. How can the United States project force outside of our borders without the supplies to back the force? The MSC operates tankers and supply ships to support the U.S. Navy fleet, provides special cargo shipments for humanitarian missions, and prepositions and transports U.S. military supplies and equipment at sea.

During World War II four separate government agencies controlled sea transportation, an unwieldy arrangement at best. After the war the United States worked hard to consolidate its defense structure, so in 1949 the Military Sea Transportation Service (renamed Military Sealift

Navy oiler USNS *Laramie* is shown here during its launching in May 1995 and full steam ahead after it has been fitted out and joined the fleet. Oilers like *Laramie* give the U.S. Navy the ability to operate anywhere in the world, a capability few other maritime forces possess. *Litton-Avondale*

The 45-year old Maritime Administration Ready Reserve Force (MARAD RRF) vehicle cargo ship, the *Comet* (T-AKR-7), is shown at its layberth in Alameda, California, during July 2000. The *Comet* was inactivated in 1984, but it remains on a four-day recall to respond to a national crisis. The vessel has a full-load displacement of 18,150 tons, and utilizes geared steam turbines that generate power for speed. Due to its age and the type of engineering plant, it is doubtful that the *Comet* will ever be recalled. *Courtesy Kit Bonner*

Command in 1970) became the single managing agency for the nation's strategic ocean transportation needs. The command assumed responsibility for providing sealift and ocean transportation for all military services and other government agencies.

Military Sealift Command distinguished itself in the Persian Gulf War as the largest source of defense transportation of any nation involved. MSC successfully delivered more than 12 million tons of wheeled and tracked vehicles, helicopters, ammunition, dry cargo, fuel, and other supplies and equipment during the war. More than 230

The U.S. Maritime Administration Ready Reserve Force tanker *Chesapeake* is shown in its layberth in San Francisco, California, in January 2000. The *Chesapeake* has been extensively modified to provide offshore petroleum discharge systems (OPDS). This system utilizes the *Chesapeake* as its fuel storage plant, and specially-modified LCMs act as towboats to provide fuel lines to operational beachheads through designated barges. The *Chesapeake* is a seagoing filling station for ground operations, and can stand offshore to provide thousands of gallons of petroleum products as needed by beachhead commanders. *Courtesy Kit Bonner*

The U.S. Maritime Administration Ready Reserve Force (MARAD RRF) cargo barge carrier *Cape Fear* is moored outboard in a raft of reserve and decommissioned ships in Suisun Bay, California. The *Cape Fear*, as shown in October 1999, is one of two MARAD RRF ships that carry LASH cargo barges. The *Cape Fear* can embark up to 840 containers that are handled by a 30-ton-capable traveling crane. This vessel is under a 10-day recall provision and has the capacity to steam 15,000 miles at 20 knots. The *Cape Fear* has a crew totaling 12 officers and 20 seamen. *Courtesy Kit Bonner*

ships, both U.S. government–owned and chartered commercial vessels, delivered and returned the largest part of the international arsenal that defeated Iraq.

MSC is headquartered in Washington, D.C., and has area commands in Norfolk, Virginia; San Diego, California; Naples, Italy; and Yokohama, Japan. Additionally, the command operates more than 130 ships and several shore offices around the world. MSC is one of three component commands reporting to the joint service U.S. Transportation Command, which is responsible for coordinating all common-user Department of Defense air, land, and sea transportation worldwide. That means MSC carries cargoes for the U.S. Navy, Air Force, Army, and Marines.

The crane ships *Green Mountain State* (T-AC-9) and *Beaver State* (T-ACS-10) are moored at the Puget Sound Naval Shipyard in Bremerton, Washington, in June 2000. Each of these RRF vessels carry three pairs of 30-ton capacity cranes. These ships are on a five-day recall and could be dispatched to any trouble spot to help offload vital supplies to the U.S. Armed Forces or its allies during emergencies. Moored opposite the crane ships is the aircraft carrier USS *Independence* (CV-62), which was decommissioned in 1998. *Courtesy Kit Bonner*

A *Shughart*-class Large, Medium Speed Roll-On/Roll-Off (LMSR) prepositioning ship is shown leaving San Diego Harbor in April 1998. The *Shugart* is capable of 24 knots from a 6,653 horsepower diesel powerplant. It displaces 55,123 tons (full load) and is 906 feet in length. This ship is designed to embark, transport, and offload U.S. Army vehicles and equipment where needed. *Courtesy Kit Bonner*

The USNS *Bob Hope* heads down the Mississippi to begin her sea trials on August 24, 1998. Officials from the Military Sealift Command and Litton-Avondale worked together to put the ship through its paces and evaluate its readiness to join the fleet. *Litton-Avondale*

The command employs approximately 7,500 people worldwide, and the vast majority have seagoing job assignments. Its workforce is made up primarily of civil service personnel, but it also includes military and contractor personnel. Unlike U.S. Navy ships, civilians operate MSC ships. In wartime, the number of merchant seamen contracted to MSC can double. The command also may call up to 1,500 naval reservists.

MSC ships come in a variety of shapes and sizes, depending upon the mission they are tasked for. Throughout the years, MSC missions have changed with the needs of the military. In the past, a military sealift would have meant the troop ships would carry thousands of soldiers "over there." Today soldiers fly to the war zone, and the most vital need for sealift is fast RO/RO ships that can carry tanks, armored vehicles, and trucks.

The transition from peace to war calls for a steady progression of increased levels of sealift ships and personnel to meet contingency requirements. The progression begins with a prepositioned sealift. MSC's prepositioned ships are loaded with combat equipment for the U.S. Marine Corps and U.S. Army forces and operate around the world near potential contingency areas.

A surge sealift moves heavy combat equipment from U.S. bases to the theater of operations.

As part of the Ready Reserve Force (RRF), ships including the *Cape Kennedy* and *Cape Knox* are berthed at ports through-out the United States. Within 5 to 20 days, RRF ships can be loaded and steam toward a trouble zone halfway around the world. *Author's collection*

In the event of a full mobilization, more than 1,000 ships and 30,000 people would be employed in sealift missions ashore and afloat. In peacetime, MSC operates about 130 ships. The command is organized around five key programs: the Naval Fleet Auxiliary Force, Special Missions, Prepositioning, Ship Introduction, and Sealift. These programs represent the command's primary business operations and function as independent units—each tailored to the needs of its own unique mission

Naval Fleet Auxiliary Force Program

The Naval Fleet Auxiliary Force (NFAF) has more than 35 ships, provides direct support for Navy combat ships, and allows them to remain at sea for extended periods of time. NFAF ships perform underway replenishment services for Navy battle groups and deliver food, fuel, spare parts, and ammunition. Some NFAF ships also provide ocean towing and salvage services. The crews on NFAF ships are civil service mariners, and each ship carries from 4 to 45 Navy personnel. Civilian crews operate the ships, and military personnel provide communications support, coordinate supply operations, and conduct military helicopter operations.

In addition to logistics operations, the NFAF has two hospital ships, USNS *Comfort* and USNS *Mercy*, designed to provide emergency on-site medical care for U.S. forces anywhere in the world. The huge ships each contain 12 operating rooms and a 1,000-bed hospital facility. Ordinarily, the hospital ships are maintained in a reduced operating status but can be fully activated, crewed, and ready for deployment within five days. When fully staffed, each ship has 1,200 medical personnel, plus a ship crew of 70.

Although this dock is a tight squeeze, we can see that the rear cargo ramp of the USNS *Bob Hope* is designed to handle tanks, trucks, trailers, or any other wheeled vehicle. Another RO/RO ramp is built into the ship's side. *Litton-Avondale*

Special Missions Program

The Special Missions Program is the smallest of MSC's five programs and is comprised of about 30 ships. It is the only program not involved in delivering materiel or cargo. Special Mission ships carry out a variety of duties that include oceanographic surveys, missile tracking, coastal surveys, cable laying and repair, deep submergence rescue support, and other unique Navy operations. Special Mission ships are either U.S. government–owned or chartered vessels and are operated by civil service mariners or mariners employed by companies under contract to MSC. Military and civilian scientists and technicians carry out the unique missions of various types of ships. Special Mission ships provide highly specialized support services and

often work in some of the most remote areas in the world.

Prepositioning Program

The successful deployment of U.S. military forces depends on the ability to act quickly. When an overwhelming force is arrayed in a swift manner, wars can be won or discouraged from the beginning. In an unstable world where regional hostilities can break out at any time, MSC's prepositioned ships provide the tools for a fast military response by U.S. forces. The Prepositioning Program has 32 strategically located ships loaded with military equipment and supplies for the U.S. Army, Air Force, Navy, and Marine Corps.

In addition to its fully activated at-sea ships, the MSC Prepositioning Program includes two aviation logistics support ships, the SS *Wright* and SS *Curtiss*. These ships provide mobile maintenance facilities for Marine Corps aircraft. Both ships are maintained in a reduced-operating status and can be fully activated in five days. (For more information on the prepositioning program, see the sidebar on Diego Garcia on the opposite page.)

Ship Introduction Program

The Ship Introduction Program is responsible for managing MSC's ship purchases, including ship transfers from the Navy, new ship construction, and conversions of existing ships. The Ship Introduction Program is especially important since MSC is continuing to acquire Combat Logistics Force ships from active-duty Navy operation and is also adding 19 new large, medium-speed RO/RO ships (LMSRs) by 2001.

The new LMSRs are a part of a strategic sealift enhancement program approved by Congress after the Persian Gulf War. Several of these ships were

Diego Garcia–The Navy's Indian Ocean Supply Depot

More than 400 miles from the nearest inhabited land and 20,000 miles from the United States lies Diego Garcia, a small island outpost that plays a vital role in the strategic network to protect American interests around the world. Diego Garcia is part of the British Indian Ocean Territory (BIOT) that was formed in 1965 from British colonial possessions left over after Mauritius and India gained their independence. It is the largest of 56 islands in the Chagos Archipelago, which extends over 22,000 square miles in the heart of the Indian Ocean between Africa and Indonesia.

Three small islands dot the mouth of the sheltered lagoon, which is approximately 13 miles long and up to 6 miles wide. The lagoon is from 60 to 100 feet deep and is surrounded by shallow reefs. The sheltered harbor is deep and broad enough to accommodate U.S. warships and nuclear submarines. The base makes an ideal fueling stop for ships patrolling the Persian Gulf and Indian Ocean. Best of all, it's a base of operations where the natives can't say no.

Britain relocated all of Diego Garcia's native Ilois population to Mauritius in 1970. Since then, the U.S. military has had a long-term lease on the V-shaped coral atoll that stretches 34 miles from tip to tip. As a result, a classified number of American marines, sailors, and airmen (plus a few civilian employees of the Military Sealift Command) are the only residents. All residents are looked after by about 50 British Royal Navy and Royal Marine personnel.

Diego Garcia serves several purposes. U.S. Air Force B-52s and AWACS surveillance planes operate from the 12,000-foot runway, and the Air Force Space Command has built a satellite tracking station and communications facility on the island. It is also likely that the National Security Agency has a listening post on the island, but perhaps the most important role for Diego Garcia is to shelter the 14 ships of Marine Prepositioning Squadron Two. These ships carry the equipment and supplies to support a major armed force with light tanks, armored personnel carriers, munitions, fuel, spare parts, and a mobile field hospital. This equipment showed its necessity during the Persian Gulf War when the squadron quickly delivered its equipment to Saudi Arabia. Soldiers flown in on air transports from U.S. and European bases quickly unloaded and deployed the prepositioned materiel.

The size of the preposition squadron at Diego Garcia in the year 2000 consisted of five maritime prepositioned ships, four combat prepositioned force ships, and five logistics prepositioned ships. Smaller prepositioned squadrons exist at Guam and in the Arabian Gulf, but because of its remote location and lack of a local population to conceal saboteurs, Diego Garcia seems the ideal place to keep so many valuable and fairly defenseless ships in close quarters. The United States guards this strategic jewel closely. Aside from a brief tour allowed in 1976 while President Carter was discussing "demilitarizing" the region, no journalist has set foot on the island. A *Newsweek* writer's dateline from the 1976 trip was cryptically datelined "Somewhere East of Suez." Construction and maintenance of the base's communications equipment, fuel facilities, and military hardware are done strictly by military contractors, and inventories of the weaponry are classified. With no family members or other civilians allowed, Diego Garcia may be the loneliest military outpost in the world.

Containers, breakbulk, or vehicles can be stored on the deck of LMSRs. These ships are also equipped with a helicopter pad for VERTREP and loading. *Litton-Avondale*

built at the Litton-Avondale shipyard in Metarie, Louisiana. Others were constructed or converted at NASSCO in San Diego and the Newport News shipyard. In 1992 a congressional study discovered the need for an additional 3 million square feet of fast sealift and 2 million square feet of prepositioning sealift. Nineteen LMSRs have been added to MSC to compensate for this shortfall. Five ships are conversions from commercial vessels, and the other 14 have been built from the keel up. At a 24-knot top speed, these ships will be faster than most commercial ships.

The Ship Introduction Program also manages the Department of Defense National Defense Features (NDF) program that expands and improves the nation's military sealift capabilities. The NDF program funds the installation of features useful to the military, such as reinforced RO/RO ramps and decks and cargo cranes on U.S.-flagged commercial cargo vessels. In return, these ships must be available to the Department of Defense if requested in a ational emergency.

Sealift Program

The Sealift Program is responsible for a fleet of tankers and dry cargo ships that move the Department of Defense's cargo during peacetime and war. In addition, the program oversees MSC's activation and operation of other ships kept in reserve, including more than 90 Ready Reserve Force ships.

For surge sealift, MSC first looks to the U.S. market to charter ships. If suitable U.S.-flagged commercial ships are unavailable, and this pool has been steadily shrinking, government-owned Fast Sealift Ships or Ready Reserve Force ships may be activated.

The trend toward containerization in today's maritime industry has created a major shortage of military-useful commercial sealift ships capable of carrying the equipment vital to a modern army. As a result, MSC has been investigating new ways to contain military cargo, such as ammunition. In addition, Congress has forced the Navy to spend money on the unglamorous but necessary mission of military sealift. In the 1980s, eight Fast Sealift Ships were added to the MSC's arsenal.

While the ship is being constructed, the vehicle decks and ramps of USNS *Fisher* are visible. A new ship in the LMSR program, *Fisher* was launched in 1999. *Litton-Avondale*

These ships—the *Algol, Antares, Pollux, Capella, Altair, Bellatrix, Denebola,* and *Regulus*—are stationed at various ports on the East and West Coasts. They can be loaded and moved out to any corner of the globe within four days. They are all named for stars in the sky and began their lives in Rotterdam, Netherlands, as the first express container ships for SeaLand Service. They proved to be too expensive to operate on regular transatlantic runs, and the Navy purchased the ships in the early 1980s.

MSC's eight "Star" ships are currently the fastest cargo ships in the world. Nearly the length of an aircraft carrier, these RO/RO ships can travel at 30 knots. Combined, all eight vessels carry the equipment of one heavy armored division. They can unload their equipment in port or use lighters (small barges) to transfer equipment onto an unimproved beach or shore. All Fast Sealift Ships are kept in a reduced operating status and can be activated and ready to sail in 96 hours.

The Ready Reserve Force (RRF) is a fleet of more than 90 reserve ships maintained and crewed by the Maritime Administration. They can be activated in 4, 5, 10, or 20 days. When activated, RRF ships come under the operational control of Military Sealift Command.

The RRF includes RO/ROs, breakbulk ships, barge carriers, auxiliary crane ships, tankers, and two troop ships for surge sealift requirements. The RRF ships are located in New York, Virginia, California, and Texas—close to significant military ports to provide a quick response to a crisis. Because of their configurations RRF ships are capable of handling bulky, oversized military equipment. The shortage of RO/RO ships in the U.S. commercial market makes the RRF especially valuable; however, some people have questioned the wisdom and viability of maintaining a fleet of freighters and tankers that, in some cases, date back to World War II.

For peacetime operations, MSC handles dry cargo movements with approximately 12 commercial ships chartered from the private industry. In times of war or other crises, MSC can charter additional dry cargo ships to expand its sealift capabilities. Fuel movement during peacetime is also handled by chartered vessels. About 10 chartered tankers carry Department of Defense fuel to U.S. military depots worldwide, and MSC arranges for fuel delivery to federal government facilities in remote parts of the world not ordinarily served by commercial tankers.

For nearly 40 years, MSC has provided fuel to the National Science Foundation's McMurdo Station in Antarctica where one of MSC's chartered tankers has its path cleared by a Coast Guard icebreaker. The MSC tanker project also provides fuel services for federal government installations in Alaska by chartering tugs and barges that deliver fuel to remote sections of the state in large, floating plastic bladders.

The USNS *Comfort* is one of two hospital ships operated by the Military Sealift Command. This 250 bed floating hospital is staffed by 956 medical personnel and a 258 member support staff, and provides medical and surgical services to U.S. Military forces and other government agencies.

America's success in the Persian Gulf War reinforced the need for a strong and ready strategic sealift program. In the years after the war, MSC's sealift missions have included allied peacekeeping missions and disaster relief operations. These quasi-military operations will likely continue, while the new and converted sealift ships in MSC's inventory will ensure that the United States can respond quickly and powerfully to any future crisis. This is just one more example of the keen importance that cargo ships play in the events that dominate world history and today's headlines.

Sgt. William R. Button is 1 of 16 maritime prepositioning ships in the Military Sealift Command Fleet. These ships are always at sea, ready to deploy equipment, fuel, and supplies on short notice to U.S. Military forces.

As the United States continues to reduce the size of its military in the twenty-first century, sealift will be an enduring mission, and U.S. forces will have fewer overseas bases from which to operate. Military readiness and rapid response capabilities will depend increasingly on maintaining a presence "Forward . . . From the Sea," which is MSC's motto. One possible shape that future sealift ships may take is the twin-hulled catamaran. Incat, an Australian firm, is proposing a 360-foot catamaran capable of carrying 50 tanks or helicopters at 60 knots.

USNS *Gilliland* is one of the MSC's 19 large RO/RO ships. Converted from a commercial container ship in 1997, the *Gilliland* transports helicopters, tanks, and other wheeled and tracked military vehicles at speeds up to 24 knots. The ship is also equipped with large deck cranes for lift-on/lift-off operation.

CHAPTER SIX

Bulk Cargo Ships

Any consumer who has shopped at Sam's Club or any similar warehouse retail outlet knows how much money can be saved by buying goods in bulk. The same result applies to shipping items such as rice, wheat, coal, and cement across the ocean. It's cheaper to ship in bulk. Besides, some cargoes just don't fit in a box.

Bulk cargo vessels have become bigger and more specialized in an effort to establish competitive and efficient cargo-handling tools for specific industries and markets. The economical movement of basic, unimproved commodities (which are mostly common bulk cargoes) can only be accomplished with advanced, well-adapted technologies. In the past, moving bulk cargo was often inefficient and unwieldy.

In 1950 an exporter moving a cargo of grain from the United States to Europe had two choices. They could package the grain in 50-pound burlap sacks, move the sacks onto pallets, fly the pallets into the available cargo spaces of a breakbulk liner at the end of the ship's crane, and reverse the process at the destination. Or they could charter an entire tramp ship with plywood grain bins, feeders, and shifting

When tied up in port the anchor is not needed, so a close inspection of it and other rarely seen parts of the ship (such as the anchor) is possible. While the ship is docked, most of the crew is supervising the cargo loading. The engineering team is working on any necessary repairs or maintenance that is not possible at sea. *Port of San Diego*

Loading bulk grain into a standard cargo ship such as this Swedish vessel, *Carina*, is a difficult job. Plywood shifting boards and bins have to be constructed in the holds and some of the cargo usually manages to end up wedged between stiffeners and bulkheads. *Author's collection*

boards built in the ship's holds and then load the loose grain aboard with a conveyor, pneumatic tube, or grabs. At the destination, the grain would be unloaded with similar equipment, and men with shovels would be needed in the hold to keep the cargo unloaded evenly. Both methods were time consuming, labor intensive, and inefficient.

The modern bulk carrier had its roots in solving this problem of moving cargo on and off the ship efficiently. The idea originated with ship broker Ole Skaarup. In 1954 his small New York company repaired and chartered ships for bulk cargoes.

Two floating cranes are nearly finished with the transfer of *Federal Fraser*'s cargo to waiting river barges. This type of operation is time consuming, but few alternatives exist when moving bulk cargo inland. *FedNav International*

Skaarup understood how inefficient the process was and imagined a new ship.

In a 1992 article in the American Bureau of Shipping's *Surveyor* magazine, Skaarup explained that "it seemed the most practical ship should have wide, clear cargo holds. Thus, it would require machinery aft, wide hatch openings to ease cargo handling, and a hold configuration that could eliminate the need for shifting boards. To make the hatches acceptable as grain feeders, they would have to extend several feet above deck."

Skaarup also wanted a safe ship that would be stable and seaworthy. When grain or similar bulk cargoes are loaded into a ship, they tend to pile in the middle of the hold and slope down to the bulkheads. This creates area for the cargo to shift, which can cause a ship at sea to become dangerously unstable. Skaarup thought he could eliminate this problem by building a ship with sloping ballast wing tanks at the top sides of the cargo hold. These tanks would fill the void left in a conventional hold and help stabilize the ship.

Skaarup took his idea to Nordstrom and Thulin, a Swedish shipping company. They were convinced the idea would work and with help from industrialist Marcus Wallenberg, Skaarup's idea became a $2.5 million 19,000-DWT shipping experiment and evolved into the OS design. The ship incorporated the sloped-wing tanks, aft engine room and bridge, wide open cargo holds with smooth sides, and sloping bulkheads. Conventional-thinking engineers at the Kockums Shipyard, where the ship was built, had fought with Skaarup over the lack of a centerline bulkhead and a dozen other important details; but Skaarup stood firm, and the ship, the *Cassiopeia*, was an immediate success.

Thanks to the new features, the *Cassiopeia* could be loaded at a savings of 50 cents per ton. This

Egon Oldendorff of Lubeck, Germany, is one of the world's largest bulk shipping operators and owns more than 150 ships—most of them are bulkers. Oldendorff's ships vary widely in size. *Helena Oldendorff* is a Handy size bulker/laker with five holds. The *Linda Oldendorff* is a Panamax bulker with seven holds. *Jeff Cameron, Egon Oldendorff*

In river ports, including New Orleans, bulkers will often use floating cranes to transfer cargo from the ship's hold to barges waiting alongside. Later these goods will be pushed up river and unloaded at their final destination. *Author's collection*

Mariupol is a Ukrainian bulker operated by the Black Sea Shipping Company. It sits at anchor down river from the Port of New Orleans. Ship captains will often choose to anchor off shore while the ship waits for cargo. Ships have to pay a fee when anchored at the dock.

seemingly small figure allowed the ship to save enough money to pay for its entire construction cost in 10 years, which is a monumental achievement in a ship designed to trade for at least 30 years. Soon other shipping companies wanted vessels like the *Cassiopeia*. Today nearly 7,000 ships of the OS type have been built and carry the vast majority of the world's dry bulk cargo.

As with other types of modern cargo ships, the bulk carrier has grown in size over the years. Today there are four types of bulk ships trading today—Handysize (10,000 to 35,000 DWT), Handymax (35,000 to 50,000 DWT), Panamax (50,000 to 80,000 DWT), and Capesize (80,000 to 200,000 DWT). Some of the commodities currently being moved in bulk ships include iron ore, coal, grain, bauxite, phosphate rock, salt, cement, wood chips, and fertilizer.

Any ship at sea can face danger caused by bad weather, equipment failure, or bad judgment of the captain or crew; however, certain ship types have special dangers all of their own. For an oil tanker, risk is usually thought of in relation to the cargo being spilled, and losing containers in a heavy storm is an economic risk but usually not dangerous to the vessel itself. Although with a bulk carrier, the cargo itself and its interaction with the ship can be a risk factor. By their nature, bulk cargoes are often heavy, dense, easily shifted, and react badly to water exposure.

In the 1990s a number of bulk ships sank or disappeared under mysterious circumstances. Between 1990 and 1997, nearly 100 ships were lost. An investigation by the International Maritime Organization (IMO) concluded that many of these ships had experienced a hull breach or hatch failure that had allowed seawater to flood one or more cargo holds. The study found that most ships could

A dramatic view of the OBO icebreaker *Arctic*. This unique ship can carry oil or ore in and out of ports deep within the Arctic Circle. *FedNav International*

The *Federal Baffin* is a Handymax bulker with a strengthened hull to operate in the ice of the Canadian Arctic. Its owner, FedNav International, is Canada's largest shipping company. *FedNav International*

survive with one hold flooded, but that two breached holds would swamp the engine room, break the ship's back, or cause its bow to dive under the waves. The IMO report stated that forward flooding was the most dangerous. When one of the forward holds is flooded, bulk cargo can often

Great Lakes Shipping

The American Great Lakes is one of the largest continuous bodies of fresh water on Earth with nearly 11,000 miles of shoreline and 95,000 square miles of water. It is also a vital highway for moving goods and commodities between America's principal industrial cities and the world.

Both oceangoing freighters and purpose-built "Lakers" serve the Great Lakes. The largest ships on the five Great Lakes are designed to carry bulk cargo such as iron ore, stone, and grain. Others carry cement, steel, and breakbulk cargo, including wine and packaged foods.

Weather can make navigating the Great Lakes a pleasure, challenge, or nightmare. Each season presents different weather problems, and each lake has its own features. Winter shipping is severely restricted by ice and storms. Some Great Lakes traffic continues into the winter, but ice on the water and fierce winter storms are always a problem. Strong winds, rough seas, and cold temperatures can cause severe icing on any ship. This adds tremendous weight to the superstructure, causing dangerous instability. Before the St. Lawrence Seaway closes in late December, most lake vessels lay up for the winter and oceangoing vessels transit from the seaway to the Atlantic.

From May to November, thunderstorms and fog are the most common problems. Great Lakes storms are often quick to develop and violent in their output of wind and wave. November storms are usually the fiercest, and it was a tempest that led to one of the most famous and deadly shipping disasters in American history.

On November 10, 1975, the SS *Edmund Fitzgerald* was eastbound on Lake Superior with a load of iron ore in her holds. At one time the *Fitzgerald* was the largest Laker in operation, and 17 years after her launching, the ship was still impressive. A typical lake bulker with deep cargo holds separating a forward pilothouse and rear engine stack, the *Fitzgerald* was heading to Detroit, Michigan, from Superior, Wisconsin, when a fierce storm began pounding her with 15- to 25-foot waves.

After losing her radar and reporting that she was taking on water, other ships in the area lost contact with the *Fitzgerald* just north of Whitefish Bay in Michigan's Upper Peninsula. Some debris was found the next day, and none of the 29 crew members survived. No one knows for certain what caused the sinking, but the ship's hatches were known to be leaking after they left port. One theory states that as the storm intensified, the cargo holds took on more and more water, causing the *Fitzgerald* to list. Perhaps the ship nosed under a great wave and was unable to recover.

The "Wreck of the Edmund Fitzgerald" is a song made famous in the 1970s by Canadian Gordon Lightfoot. The lives of 372 men were claimed in the wrecks of 23 other ships during November storms in the twentieth century on the Great Lakes. Despite the danger, ships registered in more than 60 countries

visit Great Lakes ports annually. More than 800 ocean vessels transit the lakes each season bound for American or Canadian harbors.

The Great Lakes trade has spawned a number of unique ship designs. The "self-unloader" is among the most innovative vessels in the shipping industry today. Special conveyor belts and loading booms allow the ship to perform unloading operations that are impossible with ordinary bulk carriers.

Although many different components and a crew of skilled personnel are necessary for the smooth operation of a self-unloader, there are four main features that allow the ship to discharge cargo without onshore assistance. The unloading process begins with the coal or grain in the hold being dropped onto a conveyor belt. The cargo then travels to a shuttle transfer that elevates the conveyor belt, and it is carried up to a discharge boom. The boom, which features yet another conveyor, is swung out to either side of the ship and the cargo is offloaded to a waiting barge, truck, grain elevator, or another ship. The cargo flows by gravity through a series of hydraulically controlled gates onto conveyor belts beneath the cargo holds. The gates are closed during transit and opened at a controlled rate during discharge.

The largest self-unloading bulk freighters on the Great Lakes are about 1,000 feet long with cargo capacities in excess of 70,000 tons. They are diesel powered with speeds up to 15 knots. Their crew size is larger than some ocean bulkers and usually includes 25 to 30 people. Not all lake bulkers are fitted with self-unloading rigs; however, this is the norm for most of the modern ships plying these waters today.

The *Paul R. Tregurtha* is currently the largest Laker in operation and measures 1,013 feet. Christened on April 25, 1981, as the *William J. De Lancey*, she was the last Great Lakes ship built at American Ship Building in Lorain, Ohio. Operated by the Interlake Steamship Company, she was designed to be the company's flagship. No expense was spared to outfit the vessel. Each summer season, the company's most important business customers enjoy a trip on the lakes in elaborate passenger quarters. These accommodations gave her the nickname the "Fancy De Lancey."

Designed the same as previous thousand footers, she has the pilothouse and crew accommodations located at the stern atop the engine room. Power is provided by two 8,560-brake horsepower V-16 cylinder, four-stroke Colt-Pielstick diesel engines, built by the Fairbanks Morse Engine Division of Colt Industries in Beloit, Wisconsin. The engines drive two variable-pitch propellers that are 17.5 feet in diameter.

The most famous Laker is definitely the SS *Edmund Fitzgerald*, an ore carrier that was lost with all her crew in a late autumn storm in November 1975. The tragedy is remembered today as the subject of songs, films, stories, and prints like this one by marine artist Remy Champt of Traverse City, Michigan. *Remy Champt*

With so much of its hull above the waterline, we can see the draft of *Spar Opal* clearly, a 28,000-DWT bulker chartered by FedNav International. Her four cranes can handle 25 metric tons each and load nearly 1.2 million cubic feet of cargo into her holds. *Jeff Cameron*

The MacGregors on this bulker carry an important message: Safety on a commercial ship is the responsibility of each crew member, and with smaller crews on modern ships each person must know their job well to ensure a safe voyage. *Author's collection*

become so dense and waterlogged that its pressure may buckle the ship's transverse bulkheads. This leads to a rapid sinking, from which none of the crew may escape.

Improved ship maintenance was cited as the best way to avoid these disasters. A well-maintained ship should not breach to the sea and should be able to survive with one hold flooded. Skaarup and other industry professionals have suggested that the battering treatment many bulkers receive during unloading operations with grabs, jackhammers (to pry encrusted cargoes out of the hold), and small bulldozers is one factor in the damage some bulkers suffer.

One solution may be the growing interest in self-unloaders. These ships, which are quite common on the American Great Lakes (see Great Lakes sidebar on page 74), use a completely different design to operate since they require no dockside cranes or ancillary equipment to unload their bulk

Ships like the Nimet, a handy sized bulk carrier, are equipped with their own deck-mounted cranes for moving cargo into and out of their holds. Bulk carriers may not be as efficient or as speedy when it comes to cargo loading, but they make up for that in flexibility.

cargo. At the destination, the captain simply swings the conveyor boom over the dock, beach, barge, or other waiting receptacle, and then each hold is opened at the bottom. The cargo is sifted onto a conveyor and whisked overboard. As one might imagine, this system is more expensive to build and operate than a simple OS-type bulk ship. With good maintenance, however, self-unloaders can trade efficiently for many more years than a standard bulker, although it remains to be seen whether this design will move beyond the Great Lakes and into the world's oceans in great numbers.

Although they rarely cause as much notice as a tanker accident, bulk ships have had their share of disastrous voyages. The *New Carissa*, a wood chip carrier that lost power and drifted aground off the coast of Oregon, was in the news for several days in February 1999. The U.S. Navy eventually towed it out to sea and sank the ship with a torpedo. *U.S. Coast Guard*

CHAPTER SEVEN

RO/RO Ships, Livestock Carriers, and Other Specialized Ships

*S*pecialization. It is one of the buzzwords of recent decades that pervades many businesses and activities, and the shipping industry is no different. Specialized ships exist to transport objects as diverse as wine, livestock, cars, and bananas. The specialization of shipping is in many ways a testament to the increasing efficiency and innovation of shipyards, as well as the affluence of our society and the sophistication of commerce. It requires a well-developed economy to support a shipping industry devoted to one commodity, product, or cargo.

The RO/RO is one of the broad types of specialty ships. Chapter 5 described how the U.S. military uses RO/ROs to transport tanks and military vehicles, but many more ships of this type transport simple passenger autos. Hyundai, Nissan, Toyota, and other Asian car companies operate fully enclosed RO/RO ships to transport their products from the factory to markets in America, Australia, and beyond. Many of these ships are owned directly by the car companies, some are chartered, and others are still owned by shipping companies and assigned to specific routes and carry cars from several different companies.

A vehicle drives down the loading ramp on a Pure Car Carrier. PCC's give up the versatility of transporting a wide variety of cargo to concentrate on moving as many cars as possible. *Port of San Diego*

79

The *Acadia Forest* was built for International Paper in 1968 as the world's first LASH ship. Today it still carries wood products to Europe. *Author's collection*

Before the 1950s, loading cars onto a ship was a difficult task. These heavy beasts had their gas tanks emptied and batteries disconnected before they were hoisted into the ship's hold, chocked, and secured. Only wealthy people could afford to move a car this way, but American innovation helped address the problem.

In 1957 the Pentagon issued a contract to the Sun Shipbuilding and Dry Dock Company in Chester, Pennsylvania, for the construction of a motorized vehicle carrier called the *Comet (see page 58)*. The ship was unique and addressed the problem of moving cars across the ocean in several new ways. Rather than use a crane to load cars, the *Comet* had ramps so that cars could drive right off the dock, onto the ship, and into place. Loading and unloading time was decreased exponentially. The *Comet* also had a patented adjustable chocking system that locked into the deck

and a powerful ventilation system to remove any exhaust gases that accumulated from vehicle loading.

Since 1970 the market for exporting and importing cars has increased dramatically, and the number and type of RO/ROs have increased also. In 1973 Japan's K Line built the *European Highway*, the world's first Pure Car Carrier able to carry 4,200 automobiles. Today's Pure Car Carriers and their cousins, the pure car/truck carrier, are distinctive-looking ships that have a box-like superstructure running the entire length and breadth of the hull and are fully enclosed to protect their cargo. They typically have stern and side ramps for dual loading of up to 6,500 vehicles, as well as an extensive automatic fire control system. Hybrid RO/ROs have also been built to carry vehicles inside and on the top deck. As for the *Comet*, it is amazingly still afloat as part of the U.S. Ready Reserve Fleet.

Other trades have inspired ships of specific design and use. One of the most common is the refrigerated ship (reefer). These ships were first used early in the twentieth century to move fruit from South America and Hawaii. The first reefers were no more than insulated cargo ships packed with ice. In later years, as refrigeration equipment became more reliable, perishable products were carried in cargo holds, and finally, in entire refrigerated ships.

Today reefer ships are specially constructed with several slotted decks within each hold to allow free air circulation. The cargo spaces are temperature controlled, and the humidity can be tuned to hold fresh fruit, cut flowers, or frozen fish. One Danish ship advertises a range of guaranteed cargo temperatures from 29 degrees below Celsius for frozen fish to 13 degrees Celsius for bananas. Goods are most often packed in boxes and stacked on pallets that are handled by deck cranes.

Reefer operators usually fall into three categories: food companies shipping fruits or vegetables in their own ships on the same seasonal routes,

LASH barges are shown being unloaded from *Acadia Forest*. Once in the water, the barges are tied together and pushed or pulled upriver by a shallow draft tug. Like containers, LASH barges bring the sea hundreds of miles inland. *Port of New Orleans/Donn Young*

A Nuclear Cargo Ship

Although nuclear power drives American submarines and aircraft carriers, only one cargo ship was ever built in the United States with a nuclear reactor as its engine. The NS *Savannah* (NS means Nuclear Ship) was launched in July 1959 as a joint project of the U.S. Atomic Energy Commission, the Maritime Administration, and the Department of Commerce.

This image from a promotional pamphlet shows a cutaway view of the Savannah's nuclear reactors. It was the only nuclear-powered cargo ship ever built in the U.S. Retired from service in 1971, the ship awaits its final fate as part of the James River Merchant Marine Reserve Fleet near Newport News, Virginia. *Author collection*

She was named after the first American oceanic steamship, which crossed the Atlantic in 1819 with a steam engine powered by burning wood.

The ship was originally conceived as a demonstration project showing the "peaceful use of nuclear power" as part of President Eisenhower's "Atoms for Peace" program. She was designed as an experimental 22,000-ton combination cargo and passenger ship with 630,000 cubic feet of cargo space in four holds (three forward and one to the rear of the bridge). The *Savannah* had a sustained sea speed of 20 knots, which was very fast for that era. The ship's uranium reactor produced as much power as a diesel engine burning 29 million gallons of fuel.

Besides its unusual mode of power, the *Savannah* was also unusual in that it had a large amount of space with 30 cabins on the A deck devoted to passengers who were not crew members. The cabins were spacious with one or two beds, a sitting area, private bathroom, and air conditioning. There was also a lounge that served as a theater, dining room, bar, and dance hall.

The *Savannah* was considered a bulk or breakbulk carrier. Her deep holds could carry up to 9,400 tons of cargo under watertight MacGregor hatches, but she didn't look like a typical cargo ship. Her design was streamlined and sleek, with a flared bow and modified cruiser stern.

Before being retired in 1970, the *Savannah* had cruised more than 454,000 miles and had burned about 163 pounds of uranium in her reactor. She required a crew of more than 100 highly trained sailors, including nuclear technologists and engineers. Comparable conventional ships required only 20 to 30 hands. The death knell for the *Savannah* and nuclear cargo ships came when the U.S. Department of Defense, a major customer of U.S.-flagged ships, concluded that oil-fired freighters were more cost-effective than nuclear ships. The NS *Savannah* was deactivated in 1971 and is now moored without her reactor at the Patriots' Point National Maritime Museum in South Carolina.

Other countries have experimented with nuclear commercial ships. The former Soviet Union built several nuclear-powered icebreakers in the 1960s and 1970s. West Germany launched an atomic ore carrier named the NS *Otto Hahn* in early 1968. The *Otto Hahn* was also an experimental ship built to the design specifications of the NS *Savannah*. Like the *Savannah*, it had exceptional seakeeping, speed, and performance. Unfortunately, it was also unable to post any profit because of the high cost of building and maintaining the reactor.

As beautiful as she was technically advanced, the Savannah could carry both passengers and 22,000 tons of cargo at speeds up to 20 knots. Unfortunately, it was eventually decided that conventionally fueled cargo ships were more efficient, and the Savannah was the first and last of her kind. *Author collection*

One might think that the National Shipping Company of Saudi Arabia would only be interested in oil tankers. In actuality, the company operates more RO/ROs than any other ship type. Vessels, including this one, carry manufactured goods in trailers and containers from the United States to the Middle East. *Port of New Orleans/Donn Young*

shipping companies running a two-way liner trade, or tramp operators carrying refrigerated goods as well as general cargo. The second and third types have seen increasing competition from container ships carrying refrigerated containers. With an electrical hookup, these insulated cubes can act like a miniature reefer ship on the deck of a box carrier. Some of the largest container ships now have plugs for up to 750 reefer boxes.

Because perishable cargo is easily damaged, reefer ships are some of the most carefully maintained vessels afloat, but some ships carry an even more challenging commodity—livestock. Sheep and cattle are commonly carried aboard a small group of ships converted specifically for livestock trade. Meyer Werft is probably the most experienced shipyard in creating these ships and has converted nearly 30 ships since 1970.

Most livestock ships begin life as a car carrier or RO/RO ship, but the largest livestock carrier in the world, *Al Shuwaikh,* was converted from a tanker in 1980 for the Livestock Transport and Trading Company (LTTC) of Kuwait. It regularly carries more than 120,000 sheep from Australia to

Two of the largest car-carrier fleets in the world are operated by NYK Line *(top)* and Kawasaki Kisen "K" Line *(right)*. These Japanese fleets carry thousands of cars over the ocean to the United States from Europe and Japan while exporting new and used American cars and trucks on the return trip. *Port of San Diego*

Bulk refrigerated ships carry less than 10 percent of all world cargo shipped via the ocean, but the products they carry are valuable food commodities such as bananas, seafood, meat, and vegetables. *Willem Van Maanen*

the Persian Gulf. This is a very important trade for the Middle East since Kuwait is very dependent on food imports. *Al Shuwaikh* carries its cargo on several open decks equipped with feed and water stations, as well as manure processors. In an effort to combat the excessive odor associated with so many animals, as well as to better protect them from weather, most livestock carriers are now completely enclosed. *Al Messilah*, the latest ship built for LTTC, was converted from a car carrier and retains the vessel's boxy exterior. The powerful ventilation systems used to flush out exhaust gases while cars were being loaded and unloaded were strengthened to keep the air moving and the livestock healthy.

Specialty cargoes have all types of special needs, but sometimes the cargo is less unusual than the circumstance dictating its move. Some objects that need to be moved by water are just too large and heavy to be transported by anything but a special ship, and of course, these ships exist. Heavy-lift vessels do nothing but move big, bulky objects that most people would never dream of putting on a ship. A recent example is the transport of the USS

continued on page 90

The *Al Messilah* started out as a car carrier, but now its cargo is sheep, and lots of them. This ship supplies Kuwait with a large portion of its food by bringing livestock from Australia to the Middle Eastern country. *Meyer Werft Shipbuilding*

Although they both have stern ramps, a standard RO/RO differs considerably from a Pure Car Carrier (PCC). The RO/RO's wide adjustable ramp allows nearly anything that can be wheeled aboard to be carried on the cargo deck. The PCC gives up this versatility to focus on moving as many cars as possible. *Port of New Orleans/Donn Young*

Where Old Ships Go to Die

On a remote Indian beach, thousands of men slowly dismantle the world's discarded ships using little more than their bare hands. This is Alang, a 6-mile stretch of sand along the Arabian Sea ideally suited for grounding vessels. The Earth slopes into the ocean very gently here, and through some trick of geography, the high- and low-tide marks are separated by great distances. During the full moon and the new moon each month, high tides are at their highest and ships of 100,000 tons or more can be driven far onto the beach. This allows the ships to be broken apart right on the sand without special dry docks. Whenever the tide is out, men swarm over the hulks like ants dismantling a crust of bread.

Shipbreaking has never been easy work. Dismantling a ship that was built to withstand the rigors of years at sea means cutting apart decks, bulkheads, and cargo holds. The Indian men who do the work have little training, safety equipment, or hope that they will long survive in an occupation that routinely kills one or two workers each day. The men come to Alang because the work is steady, a rare thing in India, and the pay is a few dollars a day.

The low wage is the main reason shipbreaking came to Alang in 1983. Another reason is the domestic market in India for steel, which is the main byproduct of the dismantled ships. About 7 percent of India's domestic steel production originates with shipbreaking. These ships have other byproducts that are not so desirable, however. Most of the ships being dismantled at Alang were manufactured between 1940 and 1970. They are covered in lead paint, insulated with asbestos, and powered by electrical components filled with polychlorinated biphenyls (PCBs)—all toxic and hard to get rid of. In Alang these materials are often burned in open pits or simply dumped into the ocean.

The presence of these hazardous wastes has made shipbreaking a difficult, if not impossible, task in the industrialized nations with well-regulated systems to protect the environment and worker's safety. In 1993 an environmental group in San Francisco completed a study that concluded that any shipbreaking project that properly disposed of the hazardous wastes aboard the ship would have a 99 percent chance of being unprofitable.

In India, shipbreaking is very profitable, especially when an American ship slides onto the beach. The breaking bosses know these ships will be in good condition and were built with high-grade steel that brings the best price. Other shipbreaking beaches have sprung up in Pakistan and Bangladesh to grab a piece of the action.

In response, Indian officials are talking about building a shipyard in Alang. It will use the resources supplied by old ships to put new vessels out to sea.

Many people have criticized the shipbreaking system, which exports pollution to Third World countries with every ship. As long as India and its neighbors tolerate the working conditions and environmental damage, this will be where old ships go to die.

The shipbreakers of India's Alang beach dismantle more ships than anyone else, and the trade serves as a major source of India's steel. This trade is not without its price, however. The men who work at Alang often endure horrible conditions and hazardous materials. *Baltimore Sun*

Carrying livestock can be a much more daunting task than moving dry cargo or containers. Animals need to have water and feed, and of course there is the necessary clean up. *Al Shuwaikh* is one of the largest livestock carriers ever built. *Meyer Werft Shipbuilding*

Cole from the Middle East by the MV *Blue Marlin*. The *Cole* was damaged by a terrorist bomb in the port of Aden, Yemen, on October 12, 2000. Seventeen U.S. Navy sailors died, but the ship was salvaged. In late October it was towed out of the harbor and floated aboard the *Blue Marlin*, a Norwegian semisubmersible heavy-lift ship. The *Cole* was transported to the Ingalls Shipyard in Pascagoula, Mississippi, where it will be repaired.

Different types of heavy-lift ships are equipped with massive cranes that can transport locomotives, rockets, industrial piping, and other large cargoes from dockside to the deck. Mammoet BV, a Dutch company, is one of the world leaders in this type of transport. The firm operates 13 heavy-lift vessels equipped with cranes that can lift between 175 and 550 metric tons. Other specialty ships exist to carry wine, vegetable oil, sugar, and paper.

Opposite: As a livestock carrier, the Al Messilah's holds are fitted a bit differently than other ships . . . in fact, it more closely resembles a modern dairy barn in some respects. Livestock pens, feed troughs, and water troughs take the place of conventional cargo handling gear, and everything is built to be easily cleaned once the cargo is unloaded.

RO/ROs get their name from the fact that they can accommodate roll-on/roll-off vehicles, as well as loaded containers. As this cutaway shows, RO/ROs are some of the most versatile ships on the ocean. Combo ships like this are often built to handle specific types of liner trade between preplanned geographic areas. *ACL*

Glossary

Abaft: A point beyond the midpoint of a ship's length, toward the rear or stern.

Aft: Movement toward the stern of a ship.

American Bureau of Shipping: A U.S. classification society that certifies seagoing vessels will comply with the standardized rules regarding construction and maintenance.

Astern: Behind a vessel or movement in a reverse direction.

Athwartships: A direction across the width of a vessel.

BAF: Bunker Adjustment Factor. Used in contracts to compensate steamship lines for fluctuating fuel costs. Sometimes called Fuel Adjustment Factor (FAF).

Ballast: Heavy substances loaded by a vessel to improve stability, trimming, sea-keeping, and to increase the immersion at the propeller.

Barge: Flat-bottomed boat designed to carry cargo on inland waterways, usually without engines or crew accommodations. Barges can be lashed together and either pushed or pulled by tugs and can carry cargo of 60,000 tons or more. Small barges for carrying cargo between ship and shore are known as lighters.

Beam: The width of a ship.

Bill of lading (B/L): A document that establishes the terms of a contract between a shipper and a transportation company. It serves as a title, a contract of carriage, and a receipt for goods.

Boatswain (bosun): The highest unlicensed rating in the deck crew who has immediate charge of all deck hands and who is under the direct orders of the master or chief mate or mate.

Bow thrusters: A propeller at the lower sea-covered part of the bow of the ship that turns right angles to the fore-and-aft line and to provide transverse thrust as a maneuvering aid.

Breakbulk vessel: A general, multipurpose, cargo ship that carries cargoes of nonuniform sizes, often on pallets, resulting in labor-intensive loading and unloading.

Bulk carrier: A ship specifically designed to transport vast amounts of cargoes such as sugar, grain, wine, ore, chemicals, liquefied natural gas, coal, and oil.

Bulkhead: A name given to any vertical partition that separates different compartments from one another.

Chandler: A person who deals with the selling of food and supplies to ships.

Charterer: The person who is given the use of the whole carrying capacity of a ship for the transportation of cargo or passengers to a stated port for a specified time.

Charter party: A contractual agreement between a ship owner and a cargo owner, usually arranged by a broker, where a ship is chartered (hired) either for one voyage or a period of time.

Chief engineer: The senior engineer officer responsible for the upkeep of the main and auxiliary machinery and engine on board the ship.

Chief mate: The officer in the deck department who is second in command of a ship and is next to the master, especially dealing with navigation. The chief mate assumes the position of the master in the master's absence.

Classification society: Worldwide societies that arrange inspections of ships and advise on the hull and machinery of a ship design.

Clean ship: Refers to a tanker that has its cargo tanks free of traces of dark, persistent oils that remain after carrying crude oil and heavy fuel oils.

Cross trades: Foreign-to-foreign trade carried by ships from a nation other than the two trading nations.

Deadweight carrying capacity (DWCC): A common measure of ship carrying capacity. The number of tons (2,240 pounds = 1 ton) of cargo, stores, and bunkers that a vessel can transport. It is the difference between the number of tons of water a vessel displaces "light" and the number of tons it displaces when submerged to the ship's deep load line. A vessel's deadweight cargo capacity is less than its total deadweight tonnage (DWT). DWT is the difference in weight between a vessel when it is fully loaded and when it is empty, measured by the water it displaces. This is the most common, and useful, measurement for shipping as it measures cargo capacity.

Deck officer: As distinguished from engineer officer, refers to all officers who assist the master in navigating the vessel when at sea, and supervise the handling of cargo when in port.

Double bottom: General term for all watertight spaces contained between the outside bottom plating, the tank top, and the margin plate. The double bottoms are subdivided into a number of separate tanks, which may contain boiler feed water, drinking water, fuel oil, and ballast.

Draft: The depth of a ship in the water. The vertical distance between the waterline and the keel. In the United States it is expressed in feet, elsewhere in meters.

Federal Maritime Commission (FMC): Authorizes tariffs and rate-making procedures on conferences operating in the United States.

FEU: Stands for 40-foot equivalent units, a measurement unit for containers. It's less common than TEU.

Forecastle: Pronounced "foksul." The raised part at the forward end of a ship's hull. The inside space may be used for crew accommodations or quarters, although on new ships this space is often used for the storage of paints, tackle, deck and engine stores, and tarpaulins.

Gangway: A narrow, portable platform used as a passage by persons entering or leaving a vessel moored alongside a pier or quay.

Gross registered tons: A common measurement of the internal volume of a ship with certain spaces excluded. One ton equals 100 cubic feet; the total of all the enclosed spaces within a ship expressed in tons each of which is equivalent to 100 cubic feet.

Grounding: Deliberate contact by a ship with the bottom while she is moored or anchored.

Hague rules: Code of minimum conditions for the carriage of cargo under a bill of lading.

Helm: A tiller or wheel generally installed on the bridge or wheelhouse of a ship to turn the rudder during maneuvering and navigation. It is the steering wheel of the ship.

Inert gas system: A system to prevent an explosion in the cargo tanks of a tanker by replacing the cargo, as it is pumped out, by an inert gas, which is often the exhaust of the ship's engine. The system is designed to keep fuel vapor from igniting in the tank as the petroleum cargo is being unloaded.

INMARSAT: International Maritime Satellite System.

Integrated tug barge: A large barge about 600 feet long and with a 22,000-ton cargo capacity. It is integrated from the rear on to the bow of a tug purposely constructed to push the barge.

International load line certificate: A certificate that gives details of how deep in the water a fully loaded ship can sit and states the ship has been surveyed and the appropriate load lines marked on her sides. This certificate is issued by a classification society or the Coast Guard.

INTERTANKO: A consortium of independent tanker owners that represents the views of its members internationally.

Keel: The spine of the ship. The lowest longitudinal beam of a vessel.

Knot: Unit of speed in navigation that is equal to the rate of 1 nautical mile (6,080 feet or 1,852 meters) per hour.

LASH (see also *lighter*): Lighter aboard ship.

Lay-up: Temporary cessation of trading operations by a ship during a period when there is a surplus of ships in relation to the level of available cargoes. This surplus, known as "overtonnage," has the effect of depressing freight rates to the extent that some ship owners no longer find it economical to trade their ships, preferring to lay them up until there is a reversal in the trend.

Lighter: General name for a broad, flat-bottomed boat used to transport cargo between a vessel and shore. The distinction between a lighter and a barge is more in the manner of use than in equipment. The term *lighter* is used with a short-haul vessel in connection with loading and unloading operations in harbor. The term *barge* is more often used when the cargo is being carried to its destination over a long distance.

Load factor: Percentage of cargo or passengers carried (e.g., 4,000 tons carried on a vessel of 10,000 tons capacity has a load factor of 40 percent).

Main deck: The main continuous deck of a ship running from fore to aft, the principle deck, the deck from which the freeboard is determined.

Manifest: A document containing a full list of the ship's cargo; extracted from the bills of lading.

Maritime Administration (MARAD): Oversees subsidy programs to the U.S. Merchant Marines and assigns routes to subsidized liners.

National Cargo Bureau: A private organization with representatives throughout the main harbors in the United States. It inspects cargoes of a hazardous nature and issues certificates that are automatically approved by the Coast Guard.

Net tonnage: Equals gross tonnage minus deductions for space occupied by crew accommodations, machinery, navigation equipment, and bunkers. Canal tolls are based on registered net tonnage.

Nonconference line: A shipping line that operates on a route served by a liner conference but is not a member of that conference.

OBO ship: A multipurpose ship that can carry ore, heavy dry bulk goods, and oil. Although they are more expensive to build, OBO ships ultimately are more economical because they can make return journeys with cargo rather than empty as single-purpose ships often must.

PANAMAX: Designation of a vessel designed to be small enough to transit the Panama Canal.

Product carrier: A tanker generally below 70,000 deadweight tons used to carry refined oil products from the refinery to the consumer. In many cases, four different grades of oil can be handled simultaneously.

Reefer: A vessel designed to carry goods requiring refrigeration, such as meat and fruit. A reefer ship has insulated holds where cold air is passed at the temperature appropriate to the goods being carried.

RO/RO ship: Cargo ship or ferry with facilities for vehicles to drive on and off (roll-on/roll-off) via a system of ramps. Equipped with large openings at the bow, stern, and sometimes also in the side, the ship permits rapid loading and unloading with hydraulically operated ramps providing easy access. Fully loaded trucks or trailers carrying containers are accommodated on the deck.

SEABEE ship: Sea-barge carrier with a design similar to a LASH ship but uses rollers to move the barges aboard the ship. The self-propelled loaded barges are loaded on board as cargo and are considerably larger than those loaded on LASH ships.

Self-sustaining ship: A container ship that has her own crane for loading and discharging shipping containers, enabling the ship to serve ports that do not have suitable lifting equipment.

Slop tank: A steel tank within a tanker ship where "slops" are pumped. Slop is the residue of the ship's cargo of oil and the water used to clean the cargo tanks. It is left to separate in the slop tank before being pumped out in port.

Starboard: The right-hand side of a ship when facing the front or forward end. The starboard side of a ship during darkness is indicated by a green light.

TEU: Twenty-Foot Equivalent Unit. A common measurement of cargo-carrying capacity on a container ship. It refers to a common container size of 20 feet in length.

Trim: The relationship between a ship's draft forward and aft. If a ship is out of trim, it may ride lower at the stern than in the bow.

ULCC: Ultra Large Crude Carriers. Tankers larger than 300,000 deadweight tonnage. Few of these ships are still in operation.

Watch: The day at sea is divided into six four-hour periods. Three groups of watch standers are on duty for four hours, off for eight, and then back to duty. Seamen often work doing maintenance during their off time.

Index